THE HINDU CIVILISATION

THE HINDU CIVILISATION
A Miracle of History

SHASHI B. SAHAI

GYAN

The Hindu Civilisation : A Miracle of History

Rs. 650

ISBN: 978-81-212-1041-6

Published in 2010 in India by
Gyan Publishing House
23, Main Ansari Road, Darya Ganj,
New Delhi-110002
Phones : 23282060, 23261060
Fax : 011-23285914
E-mail: books@gyanbooks.com
Website: www.gyanbooks.com

Lasser Type Setting by: Rudra Computer Graphics, Delhi
Printed at : Gian Ridhi Offset Printers, Delhi

Contents

PART-II : THE BEAUTY THAT IS HINDUISM

Preface

This book is the end-product of three years of intensive research into a subject which had been stirring my mind for quite some years but got articulated only in 2006. One fine morning in April 2006, while relaxing after completing the writing of my last book on 'Jihadi Terrorism', I received a marriage invitation card. It was from an old friend of mine in regard to the marriage of his daughter. What struck me was the picture of God Ganesha on top of the card and, more importantly, an elaborate Sanskrit 'shloka' neatly printed below it.

It struck me as strange because my friend had all along been a confirmed rationalist and Marxist to whom religion was an anathema.

That was not a solitary instance. I started scrutinizing all the cards that came in the ongoing marriage season and found each one containing one Sanskrit shloka or another, the meaning of which was not easily indelible. What was remarkable was that no two cards contained exactly the same 'shlokas' or 'mantras'. It seems there was a competition among the people to hunt out 'shlokas' and 'mantras' from the scriptures for printing on their cards. That set me thinking about the seemingly inexhaustible minefield of sacred literature being drawn upon by the faithfuls on auspicious occasions like marriage. How old were these texts? How is it that even the most "enlightened" class of people - avowed rationalists, intellectuals, professionals, academicians et all - apart from the commoners, still regard them as sacred to be quoted on landmark occasions? These questions kept exciting my intellectual curiosity about the unquestioned faith of Hindu people in thousands of years old texts even in modern times.

I came across another case, which heightened my curiosity. A highly qualified young professional who was running a successful business of his own bought a plush motor van to transport his staff to their place of work. As the vehicle was taken out of the show room and delivered to him, he started a minor ceremony. Right in front of the show room, he performed a brief 'pooja', offered 'aarti', flowers and sweets to an idol of God Ganesha placed over the bonnet, before taking the van out to his office premises. The event reminded me of the annual festival of 'Vishwakarma Puja' during which motor mechanics and cottage industry workers worship their tools and instruments.

I felt that an ancient religion which permeates and encompasses every aspect of its followers' worldly life needs a close look. Being born and brought up in this kind of tradition, though not a particularly religious person in the conventional sense, I had taken it for granted without scratching my head over it. But this time round, I stumbled upon a passage from a book by a missionary named W.J. Wilkins written way back in 1887. He observed that "with the Hindu, religion is not a thing for times and seasons only, but professes to regulate his life in all its many relations. It orders ceremonies to be performed on behalf of a man before he is born, and gives instructions to his descendents, which they must follow in order that his happiness must be secured after death........To treat then, of the ordinary life of the Hindu is to describe the Hindu religion." (Quoted in *Hinduism: A Religion to Live by;* Nirad C Chowdhuri, Oxford University Press, New Delhi, 1979).

That set all doubts and hesitations at rest and goaded me to explore the mystique of Hinduism which continues to qualify the lives of its followers even in this modern or post-modern age. A tall order, considering the vastness and complexity of this most ancient religious tradition. What enabled me to take up the study and carry it forward was the invaluable support and encouragement I received at this stage from Vishwa Samvad Kendra, Patna,-a dedicated news agency with nation-wide network. The Patna Chapter of the Kendra promptly offered to serialize my projected book as it was written chapter by chapter in a fortnightly entitled 'Flash Light' being published by it. It virtually kick started my work on the book around mid 2006 and kept me moving forward steadily since then.

In fact, the very thought of instant publication of freshly written chapters in the fortnightly gave a fillip to my writing work and also kept up the pressure to go on writing without any break. On top of that, the dynamic editor of 'Flash Light' - Sanjeev Kumar—kept me piled with relevant books and literature on the subject which was of tremendous help in my study and writing. I also had the benefit of knowledgeable interaction with Sanjeev Kumar from time to time to clarify some points and sort out my thoughts on the complexities of Hinduism. It was largely with the support and encouragement from Vishwa Samvad Kendra, Patna, that the writing which began in mid 2006, came to a fruitful completion around May 2009. The three years that have been taken to complete this book may appear to be rather long. Especially when I kept on writing regularly without any break except for a brief interruption caused by an age-related surgical procedure that I had to go through. But that would be a superficial view of the matter. For any study of Hinduism in its manifold dimensions, even a three-year time span is not good enough. The celebrated German scholar, Max Muller spend a life-time in the study of this oldest living religion of the world. He, of course, had to reckon with the language problem and spent considerable time on mastering Sanskrit in which Rigveda and other Hindu scriptures were written. Anyone studying the scriptures to day has no such problem because convenient translations in the language of one's choice are available.

In regard to the basic texts, I drew upon the English and Hindi translations of the Rigveda, Principal Upanishads like Kena, Isa and Chandogya and the epic Mahabharata including the Gita. The epic Ramayana was of course easily accessible the through the 'Ram Charit Manas' of Tulsidas.

For the rest of the vase mass of the Hindu scriptures like the Puranas, I had to depend upon secon .ary sources, that is, the books authored by Indian and Western scholars. Similar was the case with collection of information on some other ancient civilisations of the world referred to in the book. The most important source of relevant material on them was Arnold J Toynbee's book on the History of Civilisations, which I had studied and taken exhaustive notes from earlier. For the rest of the ancient civilisations like the Mesopotamian, access to Wikipedia—a rich store-house of materials on diverse subjects—through the internet came in handy for study and analysis. Internet is such a great gift of modem times which has given birth to what may be termed as the knowledge society.

Unlike the one-book, one-prophet religions of the world, the Hindu scriptures are so vast and multiple that one may spend a whole life-time to study them and yet keep wondering what Hinduism is all about. To obviate this predicament, I took recourse to the easier way of closely observing the practice of the religion by the people in day to day life. For this, I kept interacting with all classes of Hindus and otherwise accessing their religious practices through discreet enquiries and observations all through the period of writing this book. It actually boiled down to making kind of a sample survey of the religious faith and practice of an average Hindu. This exercise brought to light some startling facts as noted below.

Everyone who as born a Hindu, including those indulging in a largely hedonistic life style or bragging of their rationalism outwardly, devoted some time almost every day in what may be deemed as a spiritual practice. It could be in the form of yoga of the Art of Living variety, silent meditation of some other kind, chanting of some 'mantra' or passages from holy books like Gita or Ramayan and so on. The common people with no pretensions to sophistication and nothing to hide about their overt religiosity, did regular 'pooja' of one kind or the other before starting their working day. Even those who could not, for some reason or the other, perform formal 'pooja', made it a point to pay obeisance to the idols of gods and goddesses placed in a corner of the house with folded hands and silent prayers. For this purpose, every Hindu house, from a poor man's hut to a rich man's mansion has a sacred spot reserved for idols of god they worship. The upshot is that every born Hindu grows into a religious person by inherited instinct or tradition.

The other striking find of my personal observation on survey was the immense variety of their ways of worship. In absence of any revealed text with fixed agenda and edicts, there is no uniformity at all in the way the Hindus practice their faith in normal course. Some begin their day by chanting 'gayatri' or some other vedic 'mantra', some by reciting selected 'shlokas' from Gita or verses from Ram Charit Manas or 'Hanuman Chalisa' or 'Durga Saptashati' and yet others by just praying before their idols for worldly boons or offering flowers and burning incense. In fact no two persons I talked to in course of my enquiry adopted exactly the same mode of worship.

The last part of my finding is perhaps more important. It is that although the Hindus worship many gods and goddesses, it is not at all a split worship. That is, they do not worship one god at a time to the exclusion of other gods. They worship all their gods and goddesses together simultaneously without making a distinction between one and the other. This is clearly reflected in many of their temples, ancient and modern, in which idols of several gods and goddesses are installed - together. The worshippers have no problem in praying before them all and seeking their blessings at the same time in temples or at their homes.

This has not been properly understood or appreciated by foreign scholars who have studied Hinduism at some length. They have been so dazzled by the rich literature on Gods Vishnu and Shiva and Goddess Durga or Shakti that they tend to divide their worshippers into three different 'Sampradayas' or sects. They have waxed eloquent on Vaishnavism, Shaivism and Shaktiism as three parallel cults of Hinduism. This is actually the result of the Western mindset accustomed to the analytical method of breaking up things into fragments and studying each fragment as a separate entity independent of the others. This splintering approach may have been fruitful in the study of matter or the material world but it does not work in the sphere of human spirituality. No wonder that foreign scholars like A.L. Basham, Klostermaier and others have been wide off the mark in their study of Hindu religiosity by breaking it into parts.

Western thinkers like Rene Descartes and Francis Bacon, for instance, believed that the aim of scientific knowledge was the domination of nature by man, which implied the splitting of the universe into man and nature and analyzing them as separate entities. As opposed to this fragmentary world view, the Hindu world view has always been holistic, which affirms the primacy of wholeness over the parts. In metaphysical terms, the holistic approach recognizes all divergences as manifestations of one and the same cosmic spirit. This has been affirmed in the Rigveda in the following words:' "एक सद् विप्रा : बहुदा वदन्ति" ("Reality is one, but is described in many ways').

This basic Hindu approach of viewing the whole in its parts and not the other way about adequately explains the worship of many gods by Hindus without splitting into diverse sects or 'sampradayas'. They worship Vishnu, Shiva and Shakti and their different 'avatars' believing them all to be the manifestations of one and the same God Supreme or 'Param Brahman'. All Hindu saints from Adi Shankaracharya to Swami Ramkrishna Paramhans and Vivekananda have thrown enough light on this rather less understood aspect of Hindu worship. But it is given to common, ordinary Hindu worshipper to realize it in practice in his day to day life. For in worshipping all his gods and goddesses, he worships his 'Bhagwan' or the God Supreme, who is the 'Param Brahman' of Hindu scriptures.

In the end, I must admit that my study, in course of writing of this book, has immensely helped me in understanding and appreciating the intricacies and subtleties of the religion to which I belong by birth and tradition. And apart from a glimpse of the rich treasure of Hindu scriptures, it was the interaction with common practising Hindu friends and acquaintances which has been the most absorbing and enlightening part of the mental adventure which has resulted in this book.

Shashi B Sahai

'Sanctuary',
New Patliputra,
Patna (Bihar).
May - 2009.

Introduction

This book originated in the search for the roots of a civilization which is recognized by 'sanyasis' living a life of total abstinence forsaking all worldly comforts side by side with jet-set 'gurus' teaching transcendental meditation to their western disciples in ultra-modern 'ashrams' equipped with latest electronic gadgets. It is about a civilization which is marked by recitation of hymns and 'mantras' which are six thousand years old even today during life cycle events like births, marriages, deaths etc. It is a civilization, which is witness to hundreds of thousands worshipping a river regarded as sacred on the authority of mythologies dating back to the time immemorial. In India which is the homeland of this civilization, not only the common masses but also the enlightened ones belonging to the modern age pay obeisance to river Ganga, the most sacred one, by taking a holy dip in it on special occasions. It is not really a matter of blind faith or superstition, but of continuity of a cultural tradition coming on from far off times when the river was revered as the lifetime of the inhabitants of the land.

The most touching tribute to river Ganga was paid by the most modern and rationalist Indian in India of his time - Jawaharlal Nehru. In his will brought to light after his death,

Nehru had written about river Ganga in glowing terms as repository of India's glorious part. Accordingly, he had willed that after the cremation of his body, a part of the ashes should be immersed in river Ganga and a part scattered over the agricultural fields of India. It was not out of any religious consideration because Nehru was not a religious person, but to him Ganga symbolized the great Civilisational heritage of India.

And this was not an isolated event. Earlier, in January 1956, Nehru made the following observations about his infatuation with river Ganga in a conversation with Tibor Mende, a noted French scholar from the Institute of Political Studies, Paris: - "I remember in my childhood going to the huge fairs which take place every year in Allahabad in January, and rather enjoying my self with the crowd. The dip in the Ganges had no significance to me. But I may tell you that I have always had a tender feeling for the Ganges. It had nothing to do with religion, it is a kind of cultural background; the Ganges represented so much in India's culture, history and development.. .." ('Conversations with Nehru' by Tibor Mende, Wilco Publishing House, Bombay 1958).

This again was not just an out of the cuff observation made by him to a visiting foreign scholar casually. His reverence for river Ganga was a life-long affair, which was clearly reflected in his will. Nehru made an eloquent reference to the ceremonial bath in the river by Hindu masses on Maker Sankranti day in one of his famous letters to his daughter (Indira Priyadarshini) dated 14 January 1931 sent from Naini Jail where he was imprisoned during the freedom struggle.

The letter reads as follows: "And as I set reading, the calm of the early morning was broken by distant voices and rumblings, ever growing stronger. I remembered that it was the 'Sankranti' day, the first big day of the 'Magh Mela' and the pilgrims were marching in their thousands for their morning dig at the 'Sangam', where the Ganges meets the Jamuna and the invisible Saraswati is also supposed to join them. And as they marched, they sang and sometimes cheered mother Ganga-'Ganga Mai Ki Jai' - and their voices reached me over the walls of Naini Prison. As I listened to them I thought of the power of faith which drew these vast numbers to the river and made them forget for a while their poverty and misery. And I thought how year after year, for how many hundreds or thousands of years, the pilgrims have marched to the 'Triveni'. Men may come and men may go and governments and empires may lord it a while and then disappear into the past; but the old tradition continues, and generation after generation bows down to it. *It is fascinating to think of the unbroken chain which connects us with the dim and distant past, to read accounts of these 'melas' written 1300 years ago - and the 'mela' was an old tradition even then."* (Compiled in *"Glimpses of World History"* by Jawaharlal Nehru, Original edition, January 1934)

Nehru's disclaimer about any religious undertone in his emotional link with or reverence for river Ganga is quite understandable in view of the fact that he was an avowedly non-religious person. But it cannot hide the fact that in willing his ashes to be immersed in Ganga, he was essentially following a tradition which is followed by vast majority of the people of India, that is the Hindus, as a matter of religious faith. To the Hindu masses, Ganga is 'Patit Pavani' (redeemer of sinners) because it flows from the crescent moon perched in the 'Jata' (long hair) of God Shiva. To them, Ganga is the mother Goddess worshipped as such on festival days by offering of flowers and lighting of 'diyas' (earthen lamps). A dip in Ganga on 'Makar Sankranti' or 'Ganga Dashara' day is believed to bestow worldly boons upon the faithfuls besides paving the way for their ultimate salvation.

The surprising part is that this kind of unquestioned faith in the sacredness of Ganga is not confined to the common masses but is shared in practice by all manners of so-called sophisticated Hindus otherwise flaunting themselves as enlightened rationalists. This practice of immersing the ashes in Ganga after the death of their elders is followed by all Hindu families who can afford to do it. This is believed to be the highest and most sacred tribute that family members could pay to their dead elders.

It is not only in regard to after death ritual that the river is venerated by Hindus. It is the cherished wish of many devout Hindus that they should breath their last in the vicinity of Ganga.

I know of a college days friend of mine who hired a house at Varanasi as per the wish of his terminally ailing mother so that she could die on the bank of river Ganga. His serving old father heartily complemented and blessed him for that and wished that he should also be taken to Varanasi at the time of his death. My friend complied with his father's last wish and felt doubly blessed for that. This was not an isolated instance. In fact, there are houses in Varanasi where dying old people are brought and kept so that they could spend the last few days of their lives on the bank of Ganga.

The remarkable fact is that such deep faith in the holiness of Ganga coming on through centuries of millennia has continued uninterrupted right up to modern times. This is reflected in the glory of Varanasi situated on the bank of river Ganga which is regarded as the holiest of holy cities by Hindus even today. Located between two small rivers 'Varna' and 'Asi' which flow into the Ganga, Varanasi, anglicized as Banaras, is widely recognized as the most ancient and most holy city in the world. P.V.Kane writes: "there is hardly any city in the world that can claim greater antiquity, greater continuity and greater popular veneration than Banaras. Banaras has been a holy city for at least thirty centuries. (*'History of Dharma Shastra'*, Volume IV, by P.V. Kane, Bhandarkar Oriental Research Institute, Pune, 1953).

The most abiding factor about the continuity of Varanasi as a hallowed city for over three thousand years through the ravages of history is its situation on the bank of the Gangas. It was repeatedly destroyed and ransacked by Islamists during the long period of Muslim rule. In the year 1194, the Muslim General Qutb-Ud-din Aibak sacked and plundered Varanasi and destroyed about a thousand temples. Even as Varanasi revived and large number of temples came up during the next century. Feroz Shah ordered the destruction of Hindu temples once again in the year 1376. Whatever of temple culture remained after that was got destroyed by the Muslim ruler Sikander Lodi in 1496. During the enlightened rule of Akbar, the temple culture revived and two large Shiva and Vishnu temples were built. But with the rise of Aurangzeb as the ruler of India, this interregnum in the Hindu temple destruction campaign of Islamists came to an end. In 1659, Aurangzeb ordered the demolition of these temples and building of mosques on their sites.

And yet, Varanasi survived as a sacred place of Hindu life and learning. If Varanasi continued as a venerated city of Hindu pilgrimage inspite of the scourge of Islamists, it was because it was delicately perched on the banks of river Ganga which was indestructible. It was at the bank of Ganga in Varanasi that the Great Hindu Bhakti poet Goswami Tulsi Das lived and wrote his monumental Ramayan - the 'Ram Charit Manas' -, which is still regarded as the standard-bearer of Hindu ethics and morality.

The glory of river Ganga has been forcefully brought out by a roving western philosopher - Count Hermann A. Kyserling - who traveled in India between 1911 and 1914. After visiting the banks of the Ganges and imbibing its ethereal ambience, he recorded in his travel diary: "The atmosphere of devotion which hangs above the river is improbable in its strength: stronger than in any Church that I have ever visited. Every would be Christian priest would do well to sacrifice a year of his theological studies in order to spend this time on the Ganges; here he would discover what piety means". (Quoted in '*A Short History of Hinduism*' by Klaus K. Klostermaier, One World Publications, First South Asian Edition, 2006).

That incidentally brings out the key factor in the extraordinary reverence for river Ganga coming on from the time immemorial down to the present day. And that is the religious factor. Ganga has been worshipped by the Hindus for thousands of years not really because it was the lifetime of the inhabitants of northern India but primarily because it is believed to be of divine origin. To the vast mass of Hindus, Ganga is not an ordinary river, but the very embodiment of divinity, which accounts for their unflinching faith in its godliness. Any amount of rationalization about the cultural and other secular factors cannot supercede the basic religious content in the uninterrupted devotion to river Ganga by the Hindu people from the ancient to modern times.

That also provides a clue to a relevant puzzle. There are other major rivers in different parts of the world which accounted for the rise of some major civilisations along their banks. Nile in North Africa is one such river which had given birth to the great Nile Valley Civilisation of Ancient Egypt known for its grand old Pyramids and Mummies. River Nile finds mention in the Old Testament dealing with the plight of Jews in Egypt. And so does the river Jordan which is the lifeline of Arab people living along its banks. But there is no tradition of the Egyptian or Arab people paying obeisance to the rivers Nile or Jordan as in the case of Indians in relation to Ganga.

Another great ancient civilisation is associated with two major rivers, Tigris and Euphrates in modern Iraq. The highly productive land mass watered by these two major rivers had been home to the great Mesopotamian Civilisation which dazzled the world when its existence came to light as a result of archeological excavations in modern times. Apart from their well-developed systems of flood control, water storage and irrigation, the diverse peoples who inhabited the Mesopotanian region were united by their polytheistic religion and mythologies. They were worshippers of many gods and goddesses and their most impressive buildings were big temples built to worship their gods. But there is no trace of any tradition of worship of rivers Tigris and Euphrates which provided sustenance to the inhabitants of the region.

That would go to show that mere material value of a river in the life of a people or its contribution to their livelihood and prosperity is not enough to evoke their reverence for it to the level of worship. The rationalists who attribute the Indians', or more precisely the Hindus', reverential treatment of Ganga river to its antiquity and the life support it provided to early inhabitants of the region miss the real point. They have no answer to the question why other ancient civilisation sustaining rivers like the Nile, Tigris and Euphrates did not and do not elicit similar worshipful devotion from their beneficiary peoples - the Egyptians and Iraqis. The answer lies in the religious content of people's reverential feeling towards Ganga which far outweighs the material benefits which the river bestows upon them. For, the vast majority of the people of India, that is the Hindus, have faith in the divine origin of the river. It is the absence of this religious content or element of faith in their approach towards their key rivers which explain why the Egyptians and Iraqis do not have the same worshipful feeling for the Nile, Tigris and Euphrates.

But that also can be said to be only a partial or symptomic explanation. For basically, humans all over the world are similar in their nature, mindset and instincts. If ancient Indians invested river Ganga with divinity and came to worship it, how is it that in similar situation the ancients of the Nile valley and Mesopotamian civilizations did not develop similar reverential feelings towards the rivers that sustained them? Did they have no religion at all? Were they devoid of any religious faith?

The fact is that very little is really known about the religious beliefs and practices of the ancient Nile valley and Mesopotamian people. For the simple reason that when they were conquered by the Arab Islamists by the middle of the 7th Century, all traces of their ancient indigenous religions were wiped off by the new religion of Islam. The surging tide of Islam washed off the entire civilisational past of the Nile valley and Mesopotamian peoples. It is only through archaeological excavations of modern times that bits and fragments of these ancient civilizations have been brought to light and their history re-constructed. That leaves a big gap in our knowledge of the Nile valley and Mesopotamian civilisations and the religious beliefs and practices of their peoples.

In view of the above, it may be that the ancient Nile valley and Mesopotamian peoples also had similar religious feelings towards their life-sustaining rivers as the Indians held in the past and have even now for river Ganga. May be not. We do not really know, because in their case, there has been a complete break from the past. As A.L. Basham observes, "until the advent of the archaeologist, the peasant of Egypt or Iraq had no knowledge of the culture of his forefathers." (*'The Wonder that was India'*, A.L. Basham, Rupa Paperback edition, 1981).

On the other hand, the outstanding fact about the Indian civilisation, which is another name of the Hindu civilisation, is its unbroken continuity with its earliest roots. One notable example, again in connection with the tradition of river worship, will illustrate the point. The Hindus, classes as well as the masses, even today regard the 'Sangam' at Allahabad as highly sacred because the river Ganga is joined here by the Jamuna and the invisible Saraswati. That the river Saraswati, now invisible, was well known to Rig Vedic Indians is an established fact. For there is a highly devotional hymn dedicated to Saraswati in the Rig Veda which describes her as the best and the most venerated river in the universe. The hymn also mentions Ganga as a highly acclaimed river loved by all. That would show that the Hindu tradition of river worship in regard to Ganga and the invisible Saraswati, sanctified by their earliest scriptures, has continued uninterrupted from the Rigvedic age to modern times.

That in itself is a wonder of sorts, in the background of complete break from the past in case of the other ancient civilisations. In the case of Nile valley and Mesopotamian civilisations, the break from their past was brought about by the new proselytizing religion of Islam. In case of the modern Western or European civilisation, the break from the past was brought about by the other highly proselytizing religion of Christianity. The highly developed Greeko-Roman or Hellenic civilisation was marked by pagan worship of elements of nature. The ancient Greeks worshipped many gods mainly connected with the sky, like those of the Mesopotamians and Vedic Hindus. The father God of Greeko-Romans was known as Zeus in Greek and Jupiter in Latin. But Christianity superceded them all with the result that there is no trace of nature worship in the modern Western society. In the sphere of their religious faiths and practices, the modern Westerners have completely broken off from their Greeko-Roman ancestors.

In such a background, the extra ordinary continuity of Hindu religious beliefs and practices through thousands of years is a matter of deep study and analysis. A number of distinguished scholars, starting from Max Muller to A.L. Basham along with their Indian counterparts have dwelt upon this remarkable continuity as a unique civilisational phenomenon. But no serious study seems to have been made to explain how this has come about. Especially when the world's most highly proselytizing religious systems of Islam and Christianity, which have the dubious distinction of wiping out indigenous religions in different parts of the world, had complete sway over Hindu India for centuries. The Islamists' aggressive bid to convert the 'idolater' Hindus during over five hundred years of Muslim rule is well known, as recorded in history. When the European Colonial powers took over from their Muslim predecessors, the Christian Churches, particularly the Roman Catholic Church, made a determined bid to convert the 'heathens' to Christianity. So much so that the first European colonizers of Goa asked the local people either to convert to the Catholic Church or emigrate. And yet even Goa could not be fully Christianised, what to talk of India.

As observed above, although the fact of outstanding continuity of oldest Hindu traditions has been well recognized and commented upon by scholars, it has not been adequately explained. Some foreign scholars like Max Muller and A.L. Basham have been so overwhelmed by the grandeur and richness of the ancient Hindu religious tradition that they have preferred not to delve into the hows and whys of its chequered history.

That leaves a gap in the study of the grand old Hindu civilisation. This book is a modest effort at filling up that gap.

The simple fact of unbroken continuity of ancient Hindu traditions is no big deal in itself. For tradition, after all, may become a burden and clinging to some outdated traditions may be an obstacle to progress and development. The caste system, for instance, is often cited as an obnoxious tradition associated with the Hindu civilisation which tends to split the Hindu society. But the caste system was only a *social as distinguished from religious* arrangement in the old Indian society envisaging an occupational division of labour. It was mentioned as 'Varna' system in scriptures as an existing fact of social life and was not a part of Hindu religious system. A question mark was put even on this practice of a person necessarily following the occupation of his family. The following verse in the Rigveda suggests that a person's occupation was not necessarily determined by that of his family even in those times: "I am a bard, my father is a physician, my mother's job is to grind the corn". (Rigveda: 9-112-3). And all apostles of Hindu family of religions from ancient to modern times have categorically rejected caste-based distinctions between man and man.

In any case, the continuity of social traditions not sanctified by religion is not the subject matter of this study.

Having touched upon the fact of unprecedented continuity of Hindu religious tradition the next connected topic of this study is its relevance in the modern times. How does a thousands of years old religious tradition fit into the modern rationalist world in which religion itself is in disfavour? An anecdotal reference made by Amartya Sen to the nature and scope of Hinduism in a book provides a clue to find an answer to this pertinent question.

His grand father, Kshiti Mohan Sen, was an expert on Hinduism who taught at the school which Rabindra Nath Tagore had set up at Shanti Niketan and where the young Amartya had his early education. To appreciate the point that he makes, it is worth quoting Amartya Sen in extenso.

He writes: "Since my childhood thoughts... did not attract me at all to religion, I asked my grandfather whether I should be concerned that religion did not appeal to me. He told me, "No, in fact, there is no case for having religious convictions until you are able to think seriously for yourself - it will come with time. Since, in my case, it did not come at all (my skepticism seemed to mature with age), I told my grandfather, some years later, that he had been absolutely wrong. 'Not at all', replied my grand father, 'you have addressed the religious question, and you have placed yourself, I see in the atheistic—the Lokayata - part of the Hindu spectrum.'

"I remember reflecting upon that large view of Hinduism when, some years later, I was helping my grandfather to produce and edit the English version of a book on Hinduism which he had written in Bengali........Kshiti Mohan's book brought out with much clarity the heterodoxy of beliefs that Hinduism allowed, with a rich variety of well-developed but diverse religious arguments. Kshiti Mohan identified an over reaching liberality as being part and parcel of basic Hindu approach, and saw it as one of its intellectual contributions to the world of thought", (*"The Argumentative Indian: Writings on Indian History, Culture and Identity,"* by Amartya Sen, Allen Lane, an imprint of Penguin books, 2005)

That, if properly understood, almost settles the issue of relevance of Hindu religious tradition in the modern context. For it brings out the wide and all-inclusive spectrum of Hinduism. The unique characteristic of Hinduism is that it is wide enough to include atheism, agnosticism, monotheism, belief in a Supreme formless God along with devout Bhakti cults and worship of many manifest (Sagun) gods and goddesses. It is an extra-ordinarily spacious and universalist religious system which admirably fits in with the modern pluralistic society. For Hinduism itself is a pluralistic religious tradition that permits and accommodates as many modes of worship as there are worshippers.

In that sense, what is touted as Multiculturalism in the West and Secularism in India as defining values of modernism are essential ingredients of the Hindu religious tradition itself. In fact, the present-day concept of secularism is basically an outgrowth of Hinduism in the sphere of politics. India can boast of its secular political character today only because it is overwhelmingly or predominantly Hindu, and Hinduism defines its national culture. *If at any time, Hinduism disappears from India or loses its predominance, the country will sink into the mire of fundamentalism and obscurantism, as its close neighbours, who separated at the time of independence, find themselves today.*

As regards the relevance of Hinduism in the modern times, one has only to take a close look at the Vedic texts in regard to the grave problem of environmental degradation threatening the world today. The Vedas, the oldest Hindu scriptures have, several references relating to environmental protection, ecological balance, weather cycles, rainfall and the flora etc. The Rigveda clearly makes a reference to the presence of a protective layer-which in modern terms is known as the Ozone layer- that filters the harmful rays of the sun and protects the earth. A hymn in the Rigveda prays to the 'Ashwins' to protect the earth against excessive solar flares. Many Rig Vedic hymns describe the 'dyaus' or heavens and 'prithvi' or earth together as 'Dyava Prithvi' in glorious terms, which obviously includes the 'Paryavaran', that is atmosphere and environment, which lies between the two. Not only that, there is a Vedic hymn, quoted below, which calls upon the people in clear terms to protect the environment: "Do not harm the environment; do not harm the water and the flora; earth is my mother, I am her son; may the waters remain fresh, do not harm the waters. .. .."

The content of this ancient Vedic hymn is strikingly modern. Its ring and tone can be sweet music to the present-day environmentalists seriously concerned about growing environmental degradation and water pollution. It is a wonder that the Rigveda, which is the earliest Hindu scripture and acknowledged as the oldest religious text in the world still regarded as sacred, dwells upon a phenomenon which is typically modern. Hinduism, which traces its origin to the Rigveda, has thus the unique distinction of being the oldest living religion in the world and also the most modern.

This is true not only in the sphere of thoughts and ideas, but also in the way it is lived and practiced by millions of its followers. "Hinduism may be the most ancient of the religious on earth," writes Klaus K Klostermaier, "it is also very young and full of exuberant life." ('A Short History of Hinduism, One World Publications, First South Asian Edition, 2006). And it shows in the life and practices of present-day Hindus. Equipped with all the gadgets and facilities of modern world - laptop, internet etc all in working life, they carry on with their temple visits, fasting and feasting and holy bath in sacred rivers on numerous auspicious occasions with great religions fervour. The Hindu homes of all classes - the rich and poor - have a sacred corner for idols of their Gods to be worshiped every day. Most of the well-do-do houses have a little temple or 'Pooja Ghar' of their own where regular 'Pooja' is performed by members of the house-hold.

Everyone, from the big business tycoons to information technology professionals, highly successful physicians, surgeons, bureaucrats, top politicians down to middle level computer programmers, college and school teachers and office clerks begin to their day by offering prayers to their Gods in some form or the other. It may be in the form of chanting some Vedic 'Mantra', or recital from religious texts like the Gita or Ramayan or offering flowers and burning of incense before the idols of Gods in their homes. Launching of any new enterprise by business people is followed by special 'Poojas' at the site of the factory or business premises. Even some sophisticated agnostics leading hedonistic lives, ala the 'charavaka' philosophy, practise yoga under the Art of Living programme sponsored by a celebrated modern Hindu Guru.

The commoners, of course, worship their idols in day to day life and also objects of nature considered sacred like rivers and trees on every auspicious occasion. It is said that there are not enough days in a Calender year to accommodate the large number of auspicious days calling for religious celebration of one kind or another. Being the oldest living religion with unbroken continuity, Hinduism abounds in grand mythologies which are the source of all Hindu festivals. In Bengal, even the cadres of the dominant Marxist Party celeberate Durga Puja with great enthusiasm and fervour.

In the case of another major religion, the over-powering influence of their faith has led a section of its followers to fundamentalism and obscurantism which hamper their progress and development. How is it that this has not happened in case of the followers of Hinduism inspite of their overwhelming religiousity in day to day life? This is a pertinent question which needs a satisfying answer. But before that, how have the Hindu people, with their rather queer religious practices verging on superstition in the eyes of rationalists, fared in the modern world? To that, there can be only one answer, The vast majority of people of India, broadly counted as Hindus, have been doing quite well in all walks of modern life inspite of their excessive addiction to religion. In whatever sphere of activity one looks at - industrial enterprise, corporate management, social and physical sciences, technological advances et all - they have made their mark and fully kept pace with the people of the most developed countries of the world. In information technology and space science they have even stolen a march over many countries of the developed world. The so-called superstitious idol-worshippers have, in fact, turned out to be the latest brand of achievers and performers in every material sphere today. It has shown in India emerging as one of the fastest growing economies of the world.

To revert back to the question passed earlier, how come the religious addiction of Hindus has not impeded their remarkable progress and advancement in the modern world? The answer lies in the 'mantra' of utmost individual freedom in the matter of faith and worship which Hinduism allows to its followers. Not being bound by a single Book or a sole Prophet, Hinduism has no central orthodoxy to keep its followers tied down to any given mode of worship or code of conduct. It is not a revealed religion with the finality of its scriptures as direct words of God or His sole Prophet. As such, the Hindu scriptures have ever been open to commentaries and fresh interpretations in the light of the spiritual experiments and insights of sages and seekers in all ages. This has allowed a degree of individual freedom in matters of religious beliefs and practices which is unimaginable in any other organized religion of the world.

A Hindu may worship one god exclusively or many gods together; he may worship Vishnu, Shiva or Shakti or any of their incarnations at the same time; he may worship their idols in temples or at home; he may worship none of them but only the formless God Supreme (Param Brahman) through silent meditation; *or he may not worship at all and follow his own conscience to lead a righteous life in accordance with his inherited or self-acquired sense of morality and ethics, of right and wrong.*

Constant experimentation, renewal and individual freedom are the hallmarks of Hinduism which account for the remarkable success story of its followers in this modern or post modern age. Once it used to be said that the Protestant virtue of thrift resulted in large savings and capital formation in America, which made it the richest country of the world. It can more appropriately be said that the Hindu virtue of freedom of the individual from any kind of dogma has led the people to uninhibited progress and advancement in the material field. For individual initiative and enterprise are the prime movers of human development and individual freedom the cherished value of modern civilisation. In so far as Hinduism, with all its baggage of age-old traditions, permits complete individual freedom, it is perfectly in tune with the core value of modern civilisation.

Part I : The Great Survivor and the Saviours

यदा यदा हि घर्मस्य ग्लानिर्भवति भारत ।
अभ्युथानमधर्मस्य तदात्मानम सृजाम्य हम ।।
परित्राणाय साधूनाम्विनाशाय च दृष्कृताम् ।
धर्म संस्थानार्थाय सम्भवामि युगे युगे ।।

"Whenever there is any deline of Dharma, oh Bharata, I am born in order to rejuvenate Dharma. To save the righteous, destroy the evil ones. And reestablish Dharma, do I create myself from age to age."

That almost sums up, metaphorically, if not literally, the miraculous story of survival of Hindu Civilisation through some of the most severe assaults on it in course of its long and chequered history.

1

Through The Ages

The survival of Hinduism through the ravages of time extending over centuries and millennia is one of the wonders of history. Other religions and civilizations may justify their existence by their achievements, but the very existence of Hinduism for around six thousand years is its biggest achievement. The world has been the cradle and graveyard of many great civilizations, which have dazzled it in their hey-day, and then gone into oblivion. History has been a mute witness to the rise and eventual eclipse of many civilizations in different parts of the world through the ages, which have now become a part of history. In this background, it is nothing short of a miracle that the great Hindu Civilisation has remained intact setting the tone of the lives and thoughts of the people of India right up to this day. That is the marvel, which is Hinduism. More about it later. First a passing reference to some of the known civilizations of ancient times which are no more than relics of a vanished past.

Crete in the Aegean Basin, situated between Greece in its North and Egypt in the South, was the seat of a thriving civilization founded by non-Greek Minoans. The civilized Minoans were over-whelmed and replaced by less civilized

Mycenaens in course of time. The Mycenaens occupied Knossos, the capital of Minoan Crete, and settled down among the people they had overpowered. They mingled with the Minoans and imbibed and absorbed part of the Minoan civilization giving birth to a grand Minoan-Mycenaen civilization in Crete around 4000 years ago.

The edifice of the Minoan-Mycenaen civilization was shattered by the tough warriors from Greece who attacked and sacked Knossos, the capital of Crete, around 1500 B.C., that is, about 3,500 years ago. That was the beginning of the end of this great ancient civilization. By the 12th century B.C. the Greeks poured into Crete in floods of migration devastating Mycenae and other centres of the Mycenaen civilization. After nearly 400 years of anarchy in the Aegean Basin consequent upon constant conflict between low-land farmers and high-land shepherds among the migrant Greeks, peace was restored by around the 8th century B.C. And that brought about the rise of the Ancient Greek or Hellenic civilization, which lasted till the rise of Christianity in the Western world.

The Greeks were eventually superceded by the Romans in terms of political power by the beginning of the Christian era. But Hellenism or Greeko-Roman civilization continued to encompass Europe, largely through the rise of the Roman Empire, for a couple of centuries more after the birth of Christianity. In the inexorable march of history, the Romans were demolished by some North European tribes like Goths, Vandals and Huns. While the Romans as the dominant power in Europe, as Greeks earlier, were destroyed by the above North European "barbarians", as these tribes came to be called, Romanism as the last vestige of the Grand Greeko-Roman or Hellenic civilization was demolished by Christianity. Thus the revealed monotheistic religion of Christianity superceded and obliterated, in the words of Arnold Toynbee, "the world's collective human power symbolized in the Goddess Rome and the God Caesar" (Arnold J. Toynbee, *Hellenism. The History of a Civilization*, 1959)

Hellenism or Greeko-Roman civilization which lasted from around 8th century B.C. to 7th century A.D. and which encompassed Europe round the shores of the Black Sea and the Mediterranean as well as the Atlantic coast of North Africa, had striking similarities with the Ancient Hindu civilization of India. The common religion of the Greek city-states was worship of not one but many Gods and Goddesses. Their early Gods were chiefly connected with the sky like the early Hindu Vedic Gods - Indira, Varuna and Maruts. They had a rich mythology like the beautiful mythology of old Hinduism. Above all, they believed in robust humanism, which put the natural, and the human above the supernatural and theological. The Hellenic philosopher Protogoras summed it up when he observed that "man is the measure of all things."

Here also, there is a degree of similarity between the two ancient civilizations. The core of Hellenic Civilization was the primacy of this-worldiness as against other-worlddiness or obsession with life after death, in the lives and activities of Greeko-Romans. Although belief in the other world or life after death is a part of Hinduism, as in case of most other religions, it has never been the prime mover of Hindu life since the time of the Vedas. It is true that 'moksha' (salvation), that is liberation from the cycle of birth and death, is the distant or ultimate goal of Hindu life. But no more. And its achievement has been hedged in with such a forest of conditionality that it has come to be taken as nearly unattainable. On the other hand, the elaborate sacrificial rituals of the Vedas are meant to secure prosperity and happiness to the Hindus in this life and this world.

Even Gita, which is generally opposed to the ritualist tradition of the Vedas, affirms the value of ritual sacrifices in terms of worldly prosperity of human beings. It says: "After creating living beings with sacrifices, the creator (Prajapati) said of old: You will pro-create yourself through this....with this you will prosper the Gods and let the Gods prosper you. From this mutual prospering you will attain the highest welfare. Prospered by sacrifices, the Gods will give you the enjoyments you desire." (*Quoted in Hinduism, a Religion to live By,*" Nirad C. Choudhuri,]979) Needless to say, the principal objective of Hindu religiosity, right from the ritualistic sacrifices of the Vedic era down to diverse modes of worship of Gods in the present times, is this-wordly well-being and satisfaction. Hinduism in the most general sense reinforces human strength in facing the vicissitudes of life and is a great sustainer of worldly life in India.

Here is an illustration of practising Hinduism in our own time. I know of an elderly lady who is a devout Hindu, strict vegetarian, fasting once a week, not taking a morsel of food before offering 'bhog' to the idol of Ram, visiting every holy place in the country from Badrinath-Kedarnath in the North to Guruvayur in the South, and not missing a holy bath in different rivers across the country on every holy occasion. When I once light-heartedly complemented her by saying that she was bound to attain moksha' (salvation) by virtue of her devotion to religion, she promptly corrected me. No, she said, she didn't want 'moksha'; she wanted many more lives to live. That is the robust this- wordliness of living, which Hinduism shares with the ancient Greeko-Roman civilization.

But that is only one fringe attribute of Hinduism, which is too wide a religious phenomena to be identified with it. From the ancient Vedic religion of worship of nature Gods and sacrificial rituals through the upanishadic concept of the 'atman' or World Soul, Vedantic philosophy of integral unity of the Human Soul with the Ultimate Reality, Epic or Puranic Hinduism of Ramayan and Mahabharata, to post-epic devotional cults of Vaishnavism and Shaivism, Hinduism is a big umbrella which shelters large number of faiths, philosophies and cults rooted in the soil of India. It is like a vast ocean with diverse forms of worship, beliefs and philosophies flowing and mingling into it as its tributaries. And it is continually developing and regenerating itself. As one writer has put it, "It has aptly been compared to a Banyan tree that constantly sends forth new shoots that develop into trunks from which other roots originate to form other trunks, and so forth. The Banyan tree simile not only illustrates the diversity but also the inter-connectedness of the countless forms under which Hinduism appears." (Klaus K.Klostermaier, *A Short History of Hinduism,* 2006).

To elaborate it further, Hinduism is not only a religious faith in the narrow sense of the term. It is much more than that. It is a way of life, a view of the cosmos or cosmology, a philosophy of Oneness of the 'Atman' with the 'Brahman' (the sole and supreme cause of all things) and, of course, an umbrella religion embracing all other faiths emerging in the land of India. As such it can only be described as a whole civilization - the great Hindu civilization which is the true name of Indian civilization in the same sense that the Indian philosophy is nothing more or less than Hindu philosophy. As Nirad C. Choudhuri has observed, "If Hinduism disappears at any time, the inhabitants of India will......cease to have any distinctive identity." (Nirad C. Choudhuri in *Hinduism: A Religion to Live by*, 1979).

It is this wide sweep and vastness of Hinduism, which has prevented it from being swept off by such over-powering religions like Christianity and Islam through around 6000 years of its existence. (That is tracing its origin to the composition of the Rig Veda, which, incidentally, is acknowledged as the oldest religious scripture, and in fact the oldest literary work, in the world. The vast mass of Hindus regard the Vedas as the revealed word of God (Shruti) handed down from generation to generation to the 'Rishis' or holy men who composed them.) During this long period, any number of ancient civilizations characterized by diverse religious faiths were wiped out primarily by the highly proselytizing organized religions of Christianity and Islam.

As mentioned earlier, the Hellenic or Greeko-Roman civilization which encompassed the Western world as well as parts of Central Asia and the Atlantic coast of North Africa for around 1500 years (from 8th century B.C. to 7th Century A.D.) was eventually devoured by Christianity. When Christianity itself went through a great upheaval beginning the 16th century, leading to a split between the Catholic church and various Protestant sects, some of the secular values of the old Greeko-Roman civilization like its robust humanism and this-worldiness were resurrected by the Europeans. This revival of interest in the Greek and Latin literature and value-systems of the Greeko-Romans from the 16th century onwards came to be known as the European "Renaissance". But it remained confined to secular or non-religious matters. They appreciated the beauty of the classical or pagan works but not the nature worship of the Greeko-Romans. The Pagan (nature worship) and polytheistic (worship of many Gods) religion which characterized the ancient Greeko-Roman civilization was completely polished off or erased by Christianity. In such a backdrop, its a wonder that Hinduism or Hindu civilization which is much older than Greeko-Roman civilization, is still alive and continues to shape the lives and conduct of the vast majority of the people of India.

2

End of Civilisations

While the Hellenic or Greeko-Roman civilisation, the most well known and documented among the ancient civilisations of the world, was swept off by Christianity, some of the other ancient civilisations were completely wiped out by the other highly proselytizing religion of Islam. The Mesopotamian civilisation, one of the oldest known civilisation of the world, is the most glaring example of burial of ancient civilisations into the graveyard of history.

Mesopotamia is the Greek name given to the geographical area between the rivers Tigris and Euphrates comprising the modern Iraq with parts of eastern Syria and southern Turkey. The fertile land mass watered by these two rivers has often been called "the cradle of civilisation" because of its well developed technologies of flood control, water storage, and irrigation, its mathematics, astronomy and polytheistic religion. Mesopotamia had been home to many ancient peoples like Sumerians, Akkadians, Babylonians and Assyrians who all contributed their bit to the ancient Mesopotamian civilisation.

But the major component of the Mesopotamian civilisation was of Sumerian origin. Sumer was the southernmost part of the alluvial plains between the rivers Euphrates and Tigris and its inhabitants are believed to be the earliest people to have lived and prospered in this region. Akkad was the land in central Mesopotamia around modern Baghdad inhabited by a semetic people known as the Akkadians. They had conquered the Sumerians for a time but had been beaten back. Ultimately, the Sumerians declined and were superceded by Amorites based in Babylone who came to be known as Babylonians. The Assyrians, originally from northern Mesopotamia, were to appear much later to drive the Amorites out of Babylon and carry on with the traditions of the Mesopotamian civilisation.

The Sumerians were, thus, not only the earliest known inhabitants of Mesopotamia but also the foundation - layers of what has come to be known as the Mesopotamian civilisation. Thousands of clay tablets written upon in a cuneiform writing system buried deep under the ruins of ancient cities were of Sumerian origin. It is the Sumerians who invented the picture type writing system, which is the oldest known written language in the world, and which developed into the cuneiform writings of clay tablets. It is these clay tablets discovered in archeological excavations in modem times which are the greatest source of knowledge about the Mesopotamian civilisation. Thousands of inscriptions on clay tablets including hymns and prayers provide a clue to the religious and cultural life of Mesopotamia in the hoary past. Even when the Sumerians were superceded by the Amorite Babylonians as the ruling race, they preserved most of the Sumerian culture and Sumerian continued to be the language of religion and culture.

The most important component of Mesopotamian civilisation was its religion which threaded together the diverse peoples and races that came to occupy the centre-stage in

Mesopotamia at one time or the other. Like Hinduism which has joined together the diverse linguistic and regional groupings since the time immorial to give India its distinctive identity, the Mesopotamian religion, which again was largely of Sumerian origin, defined and characterized the ancient Mesopotamian civilisation. For religion has ever been the most abiding factor in social and individual life of man. If religion is taken out of consideration, the Mesopotamian identity itself would disappear, disintegrating into diverse, scattered life styles, languages and cultures of Sumerians, Akkadians, Babylonians and Assyrians.

The Mesopotamian religion was essentially polytheistic, that is they believed in not one but many Gods. Although the beliefs were common in the whole of Mesopotamia, different city states had their own Gods, temples and priest - kings. The Sumerian word for universe was an-ki, which refers to the God - An and the Goddess- ki. Their son was Enlit, the air God, who was believed to be the most powerful God. He was their main God, as the Greeks had Zeus and the Romans had Jupiter. Marduk was the principal God of Babylon. Ishtar was the Goddess of love and sex in Sumer, Babylonia and Assyria. Nabu was the Mesopotamian God of writing, considered to be the epitome of wisdom. They also believed in the sun God (Utu) and moon God (Nanna). Sumerian beliefs were actually the inspiration for much of later Mesopotamian mythology and religion. The most impressive and famous Sumerian buildings were the huge temples built to worship their Gods known as Ziggurats.

The Mesopotamian civilisation was wiped out not when the last of the Mesopotamians - the New Babylonians or Assyrians, were conquered by the Persian Emperor Cyrus in the year 539 B.C., nor even when the Macedonian Greek Alexander 'the Great' conquered the Persian Empire itself in 331 B.C. It was finally erased from the pages of history when the Arab Muslims entered the region in the year 637 A.D. under the Caliphate of Omar.

It may be noted that after the passing away of prophet Mohammad in the year 632 A.D., Islam jumped out of the realm of pure religious faith and became a powerful polico-religious entity identified with the Arabs. And under Omar, the second Caliph after the Prophet, the Arab Islamists set out to conquer their known world. During ten years of Omar's Caliphate, the Arab Muslims conquered the whole of Mesopotamia and Persia, that is the present day Iraq, Syria and Iran. That was the end of the great Mesopotamian civilisation. For the Arab Islamists with their aggressive monotheism - only one God and one prophet - and uncompromising hostility to image worship, demolished all traces of polytheism and worship of nature gods by diverse Mesopotamian peoples. Far from taking pride in their glorious Mesopotamian past, the Muslim peoples of Iraq and Syria would not even like to remember it. For them the ancient Mesopotamian civilisation did not exist. It was lucky that archeological excavations in modern times led to the discovery of thousands of clay tablets, which brought to light the existence of this great ancient civilisation.

The remarkable fact about Islamism as a politico-religious force, as distinguished from Islam as a pure religious faith preached by its Prophet, is that it washes all lands that come under its control clean of their pre-Islamic past. The total wash-out of the ancient Persian civilisation and Zoroastrian religion is another notable example of the civilisational cleansing up character of Islamism. The conquest of Persia by Arab Islamists in 7th century A.D. brought about the end of the native Persian Empire and Zoroastrian religion. The Persian prophet Zoroaster (Zarathushtra), it may be noted, founded the religion known as Zoroastrianism in 600 B.C., around 1200 years before the birth of Islam. Zoroastrianism remained the official religion of Persia for over four centuries beginning 226 A.D. when Ardeshir I took over as the Emperor of Persia. His dynasty known as the Sassanid dynasty had posed a tough challenge to the Romans who had assumed the mantle of the Hellenic civilisation from the Greeks. But once the Persian Sassanids were conquered by the Arab Islamists in the year 637 A.D., not only the native Persian Sassanid Empire and Zoroastrian religion but also the great ancient Persian civilisation came to an end. There is no trace of Zoroastrian religion in Iran which is the new name of old Persia. This religion survives among the Parsees of India who are the descendents of Zoroastrian refugees who fled their home land after its total Islamisation.

The same more or less is true of the great ancient civilisation of Nile Valley in Egypt. It was around two and a half thousand years before Christ that the Egyptian Pyramids were build during the Memphite Empire. After the conquest of Egypt by Alexander 'the Great', in 332 B.C. it came to be ruled by one of his generals, Ptolemy and his dynasty. Alexandria was its capital during this period and it continued to be a great center of knowledge and learning even after Egypt came under Roman over-lordship. But its nemesis came when the Arab Islamists conquered Egypt in the 7th century A.D. One of the first things they did was to burn the famous library of Alexandria which was a store-house of centuries of collected knowledge in science and philosophy. They proclaimed, it is said, that if the books were in agreement with the Quran, they were redundant, if not, they were repugnant and pernicious; in either case they deserved to be burnt. That symbolized the end of the ancient Egyptian civilisation which lies buried in the sands of the Nile, remembered only by the magnificent pyramids, Mummies and ruins of great temples.

In this inexorable death parade of ancient civilisations like the Mesopotamian, Egyptian, Greeko-Roman and Persian, the great Hindu Civilisation stands out as the lone survivor.

The Vedic religion that goes by the name of Hinduism continues to sanctify every act of Hindu life from birth to death according to Vedic rites even today. That is a feat of civilisational continuity, which only Hinduism can boast of.

3

The Hindu Philosophy

In his "Glimpses of World History", Jawaharlal Nehru writes: "Hinduism, the oldest of great religions existing today, is of course the product of India." And elaborating upon its continuity, he goes on to observe further that the old Indian civilisation is the basis of Indian life even today. As a self-proclaimed agnostic in the matter of religious faith and an inveterate secularist in politics, he just fell short of identifying Hinduism with the Indian civilisation. But the implication is obvious, that is, what he calls "the old Indian civilisation" is nothing more or less that the old Hindu civilisation. For Hinduism alone is the most important and abiding link between ancient and modem Indian life.

The complete identification of Indianism with Hinduism is most evident in what has come to be known as the Indian Philosophy, as distinct from Western philosophy. Dr. S. Radha Krishnan is universally acknowledged as the most authentic interpreter of Indian philosophy in modern times. Heading the chair of Indian philosophy at Oxford University for many years, Dr. S. Radhakrishnan made the rich philosophical heritage of

India accessible to the western world. But what did he put before the world as the core of Indian philosophy? It was out and out Hindu philosophical thought sprouting from ancient Vedanta and Upanishads. He accepted the existence of the world soul or the Supreme Absolute, that is, a primal spiritual being as the ultimate cause of all things. He also adhered to the conceptual distinction between the impersonal absolute or the "Nirgun" God and 'Sagun' God or 'Ishwara". This conceptual distinction can be traced direct to the ancient Vedanta and the Upanishads.

The Upanishads in fact are the fountain spring of the entire system of Hindu/Indian philosophy. They contain all the basic ideas from which the later systems of Hindu philosophy developed. And Upanishads are integral parts of the Vedic scriptures. Each Veda (Rigveda, Samveda, Yajurveda and Atharveda) is divided into three parts - *(a)* the Samhitas, *(b)* the Brahmanas and *(c)* the Upanishads. The Samhitas, written in verse, contain hymns and prayers. The Brahmanas deal with rituals and theology and also contain explanations of the Samhitas. The Upanishads are treatises on philosophy representing the highest product of the ancient Hindu intellect. They represent the intellectual side of Hinduism as distinct from the ceremonial side. The core idea of the Upanishads is that nothing exists except the 'atman' (world soul) and that 'atman' is everything and everything is 'atman'. This pantheistic doctrine was later developed with marvelous fullness and subtlety in the Vedanta system of philosophy. More of it later. It is enough to point out here that what is known as the Indian philosophy is nothing more than the development of Hindu philosophical tradition.

In that sense, the Indian philosophy differs fundamentally from the western philosophy which is basically mundane or non-religious. The origins of western philosophy may be traced to a class of professional teachers in ancient Greece known as Sophists. Many of them denied that men could ever know anything certain about the world or Gods or in fact anything at all. They asserted that right and wrong, justice and injustice, truth and falsehood were merely artificial conventions upheld by human societies for their own convenience. Though not a professional Sophist, Socrates came to be the most famous wandering Sophist who went about talking to the people of Athens who cared to listen in streets and market places. He had nothing to say about the nature and origin of the Universe about which all wisemen disagreed. The only question he posed in this connection was why the Universe was made as it was, to which no one had found any answer. What people needed to know, he argued, was how to make the best out of living. In the words of some western thinkers, Socrates brought philosophy down from heaven to earth. And so has the western philosophy remained all through the long course of its development.

Socrates left no written words behind him, but his tradition was carried forward remarkably well by his famous disciple, Plato. It was Plato who authored a series of dialogues in question-answer format as a monument to his beloved master. That eventually became the starting point of much that is fruitful and profound in European thought today. As one thinker has observed, philosophy (Western) ever since then has consisted largely of "foot notes on Plato". Right from Plotinus to Dante, Spinoza, Rene Descartes, Kant and Hegel, Western philosophy has remained separate from and unconnected to religion. It has charted a different course running parallel to Christianity, the dominant religion of the West, without any semblance of inter-connectedness.

Basically, this duality between religion and philosophy in the West arises out of the very character of Christianity. A revealed religion with the finality of the Gospel as the word of God, Christianity, admits of no philosophy, that is, the use of reason in seeking the truth or knowledge of the ultimate reality.

In such a revealed religion, there is no scope or space for arguments about the principles governing existence of the universe. That explains why there is Christian theology and Christian mythology (resurrection of Christ), but no Christian philosophy as such. The same is true of Islam, which is another more rigid and inflexible revealed religion. Christianity at least went through a great upheaval during the 16th century challenging the supremacy of the established church and beliefs, but Islam had none. In fact, it cannot have any, because any question about the validity of the revealed book is considered outright blasphemy and sin. Islam, therefore, has theology, but there is no such thing as Islamic philosophy.

So far as Western philosophy is concerned, it is entirely independent of and separate from Christianity, as pointed out above. The Indian philosophy, on the other hand, is an outgrowth of Hinduism itself, that is, it has its roots in the very scriptures of Hinduism. It is only Hinduism, apart from Buddhism which is its offshoot as to be elaborated later, among the major living religions of the world that has a fully developed philosophy of its own. It is this Hindu philosophy so admirably expounded by modern thinkers like Dr. S. Radhakrishnan and others which is known as Indian philosophy the world over. In this sense, Hinduism, with its rich philosophy, is cut above the rest and stands as a class apart.

In fact, philosophy, in the sense of deep speculation about the ultimate cause of creation and origin of the universe, is an integral part of the Vedic religion that goes by the name of Hinduism. It is well known that Rigveda is full of prayers, hymns and religious invocations. But it is not so well known that it also raises serious questions about the very creation of the universe. Rigveda says, "who really knows?... Whence was it produced? Whence is this creation?.....Perhaps it formed itself, or perhaps it did not - the one who looks down on it, in the highest heaven, only he knows it or perhaps he does not know."

(Quoted in "The Argumentative Indian - Writings on Indian History, Culture and Identity" by Amartya Sen, 2005). These are questions which belong to the realm of philosophy, as distinguished from pure religion as a faith in the conventional sense of the term. The seeds of philosophy can thus be traced to Rigveda itself which grew into the magnificent orchard of Hindu philosophy in ancient Vedanta.

That brings us to the vital question - What exactly is Hinduism? A mode of worship? A type of man's spirituality or spiritual endeavour? A philosophical quest to know the mystique of creation? A code of conduct? A way of life? The answer is - Hinduism is all this and more - a means of achieving supreme fulfillment of the human spirit. It has been best described by Sri Aurobindo in an observation made in August 1919 thus: "The religious culture which now goes by the name of Hinduism......gave itself no name, because it set itself no sectarian limits, it claimed no universal adhesion, asserted no sole infallible dogma, set up no single narrow path or gate of salvation; it was less a creed or cult than continuously enlarging tradition of the God-ward endeavor of the human spirit. An immense, many-sided and many-staged provision for a spiritual self-building and self-finding, it had some right to speak of itself by the only name it knew, *the eternal religion, "Sanatan Dharma"* (Quoted in.... "The Concept of Hindu Nation" by Abbas Chatterjee, 1995).

4

"Sanatana Dharma" or Hinduism: How Old?

Nirad C. Choudhury writes: "Historically, the great achievement of Hindu religion is that it has enabled Hindu society and culture to survive through vicissitudes which has destroyed other societies and cultures contemporaneous with it." (*"Hinduism". A Religion to Live By,* 1919). But how old is Hinduism? That is a million dollar question which deserves to be addressed more seriously than what has been done so far. The conventional periodisation of ancient Indian history seeks to make out that Hinduism is about 3500 years old, that is, 1500 years before Christ (B.C.). In the light of recent archeological findings and other evidences brought to light by many scholars, the time span of Hinduism needs to be re-examined at some length.

The common run of historians trace the origin of Hinduism to the so called invasion of India by the Aryans around 1500 B.C. and the composition of the hymns of the Rigveda after that. A.L. Basham, for instance, accepting the Aryan invasion theory, dates the composition of 1028 hymns of the Rigveda to between 1500 and 1000 B.C. Others put it between 1400 and 1200 B.C. and that is supposed to be the beginning of Hinduism.

As far as linking the beginning of Hinduism with the composition of the Rigveda is concerned, there is no scope for any doubt. The Rigvedic hymns are the oldest Hindu scriptures, believed to be revealed words of God ('Shruti') handed down to 'Rishis' or holy men who composed them. But the dating of the Rigveda itself by European historians of late 19th century and blindly accepted by Indian historians generally, is severely flawed. It is based on the faulty theory of invasion of India by Aryan tribes from the northwest who were supposed to have imposed their culture and religion on the indigenous people of India. Rigveda, according to A.L.Basham, "is evidently the work of an invading people" and "the forts or citadels which the Vedic war - God Indra is said to have destroyed included Harappa......The invaders of India called themselves Aryas, a word generally anglicized into Aryans." (*"The Wonder that was India"*, A.L. Basham, 1981.)

A peripheral historian like Jawaharlal Nehru has become lyrical while describing the so-called invasion of India by the Aryans in the distant past. In his famous letters to his daughter, he writes "we are in the direct line, it may be, with the ancients, who came down through the north-western mountain passes into the smiling planes of what was to be known as Brahmavarta, and Aryavarta and Bharat Varsha... Think of them, those distant ancestors of ours, marching on and on, and suddenly reaching the banks of the noble Ganga flowing majestically down to the sea. Now the sight must have filled them with joy?" (*Glimpses of the World History*, J.L. Nehru).

But is there any scientific, archeological or recorded evidence to sustain this so-called Aryan invasion theory ? A close scrutiny would show that there is none. Apparently, the Aryan invasion theory is no more than pure speculation. When

Western scholars found some affinity between many European languages and Sanskrit, or believed they had found some, and they automatically concluded that the Sanskrit speaking Vedic Indians were of Indo-European stock having arrived in India from outside. Implicit in this assumption was the vain belief of the Europeans that the superior culture of the Aryans must have come to backward India from Western sources. Abbe Dubois, a French scholar who wrote on Hindu customs and traditions during early 19th century, observed about the inhabitants of India (Aryans): "According to my theory, they reached India from the North, and I should place the first abode of their ancestors in the neighbourhood of the Caucasus." ('Hindu Manners, Customs and Ceremonies' third edition 1906, reprint 1959). But the real originator of the Aryan invasion theory was Max Muller who laid down his own chronology of the Vedas, dating the Rigveda to around 1200 B.C. after the arrival of the Aryans into north India.

Needless to say, the Aryan invasion theory and dating of the Vedas by European scholars like Max Muller was purely conjectural. The great Indian revolutionary turned Yogi Sri Aurobindo - rejected the Aryan invasion theory early in the 20th century as a figment of the imagination of western scholars. He never believed in the absurd division between the Aryans and Dravidians. In "The Secret of the Veda", written between 1914 and 191 6, Sri Aurobindo observed: "I regard the so-called Aryans and Dravidians as one homogeneous race."

The essential homogeneity of the so-called Aryans and Dravidians is confirmed by their common religious beliefs and practices from the earliest times down to this day. This is well proved by the origin and development of the two most important traditions of mainstream Hinduism - Shaivism' and Vaishnavism. The most important source of Shaivism can be traced to the ancient Dravida culture. Even the name 'Shiva' seems to have been derived from the Tamil word 'sivan' meaning red, which was believed to be the colour of God Shiva. The early Aryans called Shiva 'Nila Lohita' meaning, 'The Red one with Blue (Throat)' referring to the mythology of God Shiva drinking the poison that come out of ocean churning. Many characteristic features of Shaivism fit in more appropriately with Dravida culture of South India. And yet Shiva under his other name Rudra figures as a God in the Vedas also. Hymns are addressed to Rudra (Shiva) as one of the Gods in Rigveda and more prominently in Atharveda. In the earliest Shiva Upanishad, Shiva is identified with Brahaman, the Supreme Being. In the epics-Ramayan and Mahabharat Shiva mythology developed to its full glory. In Ramayan, Shiva is addressed as Mahadeva, Rudra, Pashupati and Shankar. In Mahabharat, Krishna, an avatar of Vishnu, is depicted as a Shiva bhakta.

Similarly, Vaishnavism is both Aryan and Dravidian in its origin and development. Rigveda Samhita contains several hymns addressed to Vishnu. To the Aryans, Vishnu was a form of Sun God identical with the Dravidian Sky-God whose colour was sky blue. Narain, the other name of god Vishnu, is of Dravidian origin. The identification of Narain with 'Parmatman' or the Supreme God speaks of the fusion of the Vedic and Dravidian deities which rules out any question of duality between the two. Although Vaishnavism is considered primarily a Vedic religion and some Brahmana passages address Vishnu as the 'greatest' God, Vishnu-Narain has been worshipped in the Dravidian or Southern India since the earliest of times. Some of the most revered Gods of the South like Lord Venkateshwara of Tirupati and the deities of Guruvayur and Ayappa of Kerala are part of the Vishnu mythology. It is absurd to think that such deep-rooted faith in the Vedic religion since the ancient times could be planted among the Dravidian people by a conquering race of Aryans.

There are other more clinching evidences to reject the Aryan invasion theory invented by 19th century western historians. There is no memory of any invasion by outsiders like Aryans in the records of ancient India like the Vedas, Tamil literature and Buddhist or Jain writings. There is considerable affinity between the archeological artifacts of the Indus (Harappan) Civilization and subsequent Indian society and culture. A continuity of modes of worship, arts, crafts, architecture etc is clearly visible in the later Indian social life. Similarly, there is remarkable continuity in the development of scripts from Harappan to Brahmi to Devnagari. Perhaps the most conclusive fact to demolish the Aryan invasion theory and establish that the Indus (Harappan) Civilization itself was Vedic is its own town planning and architectural design. These required a fairly advanced geometry of the type mentioned in the Vedic 'Sulvasutras.'

In view of the above, it is reasonable to believe that the Indus (Harappan) Civilization itself was a late Vedic phenomenon, that is, the Vedic age preceded the Harappan period. The Indus cities (Harappa and Mohenjo Daro) were not destroyed by Aryan invaders but were deserted by their inhabitants because the region was reduced into desert. Recent satellite photography and geological investigations have revealed that the mighty river Saraswati, known to Rigvedic Indians, had completely dried out by around 3900 years ago, that is 400 years before the Aryans were alleged to have invaded and sacked the Indus cities. It is evident, therefore, that the battles mentioned in the Rigveda were not fought between the Indus people and the invading Aryans but between groups belonging to the same race. Moreover, the racial diversity found in the skeletons discovered in the ruins of the Indus cities is the same as in present day India. That rules out the likelihood of coming of a new race from outside.

These evidences push back the date of the Rigveda and origin of Hindu civilizations by thousands of years. Accordingly, the date of the Rigveda and the beginning of Hinduism can be assumed to be around 6000 years ago (4000 years before Christ) and not 3500 years (1500 years before Christ) sought to be fixed by Max Muller and other western scholars. It would be interesting to note that the purely speculative nature of timing of the Vedas by westerners was hinted at by Max Muller himself during the closing years of his scholarly life. In his last work, "*The Six Systems of Indian Philosophy*," Max Muller observed: "Whatever may be the date of the Vedic hymns, whether 1500 or 15,000 B.C., they have their own unique place and stand by themselves in the literature of the world". This healthy intellectual doubt raised by the originator of the conventional timing of the Vedas and Aryan invasion theory almost nails the coffin of the theory itself.

5

The Wide Sweep of Hinduism

As discussed in the previous chapter the theory of Aryan invasion of India from outside was no more than a myth created by western Historians. The blind acceptance of this theory by subsequent historians, both Indian and western, has led to considerable confusion in understanding the true character of Hinduism and its growth in India. Once the mythical theory of Aryan invasion is set aside, the organic unity and homogeneity of Hindu civilization Vedic, Harappan and Dravidian becomes self-evident. That brings out the true picture of Hinduism, which has ever defined the Indian identity. In cultural or civilisational terms, Hinduism has encompassed the whole of India, north south east and west since the beginning of history. This is well illustrated by the legends surrounding the famous sage Agastya. legends, it must be remembered, are accounts of notable personalities and events associated with them carried by word of mouth from generation to generation. They are valuable sources of information about ancient time in absence of any written account or document.

According to tradition, sage Agastya was the 'Kulguru' (royal chaplain) of the divine line of Pandyan rulers of the South and father of Tamil Language and grammar. The Pandyan rulers of the Dravidland, it may be noted, were believed to be the descendents of god Shiva and goddess Parvati. Apart from tradition and legend, Tamil scholar of the medieval period Perasiriyar has affirmed, with support from more ancient writings, that Agastya was the original founder of Tamil language and grammar. Another story is narrated by a Tamil commentator of the middle Ages, on the authority of a more ancient writer. According to it, when Agastya came to Podiya hill in the extreme South, he prevailed over Ravana who had tyrannised over the land to leave it alone and confine himself to Lanka.

But who was Agastya in the first place? By all accounts, he was a vedic seer who took his abode in the Dravidland where he was hailed as a holyman. His vedic origin is testified by the fact that there is a brief reference to his miraculous birth from a pitcher (Kumbha) in the Rig Veda. The Agastya legends have been more fully developed in the epics, Ramayan and Mahabharata, as well as in Tamil literature (Nilkanta Shastri, *A History of South India*, Fourth Edition, 1975). That would go to show the integral unity and homogeneity of Hindu civilization which encompassed the so-called Aryan North and Dravidian South to give the whole of India its distinctive identify. It is intact even today.

Another fact which highlights the Hindu identify of the whole of India is related to the name of the holy city of Mathura. Associated with the birth, Childhood and 'Karmabhoomi' of Lord Krishna, Mathura is one of the most revered places of pilgrimage for the Hindus. And it is no mere coincidence that the capital city of the ancient Pandyan rulers of the south was also named Madhura now Tamilised and Madurai. Evidently this famous city of Tamil Nadu derived its name from Lord Krishna's birth place in Brojmandal situated on the banks of river Yamna in

Uttar Pradesh. And both the cities are as old as early Hinduism. The inter-connection between Mathura and Madhura or Madurai is established by the keen interest in and reverence for the epic Mahabharata associated with Lord Krishna shown by the early Pandyan rulers of the South. One of their great achievements was that they got the epic Mahabharata translated into Tamil. They also established a 'Sangam' or college of Tamil poets at Madhurai which flourished for a long time under a succession of Pandyan Kings as patrons.

The Mathura legend does not stop at that. There are other Mathuras across the sea in Sri Lanka and near Java in what is now Indonesia. That tells its own story. It is a very significant pointer to the spread of Hinduism in ancient times beyond the borders of India. Bali island of Muslim Indonesia has a sizeable Hindu population today. Inspite of Islamisation of the country, Indonesia still retains some of the Hindu names and symbols. For instance, 'Devi' is a common suffix of name of Indonesian women. And the national Airline of Indonesia is named Garuda Airline after the bird carrier 'garuda' of Lord Shiva's elder son Kartikeya of Hindu mythology. Even Sukarno, the name of the erstwhile charismatic leader of Indonesia, was a derivation of 'sukarna' of Mahabharat frame. The legends of the epics Ramayan and Mahabharat are still very popular in Bali and Java. Islamisation has not been able to wipe out many of the symbols of Hindu civilization from Indonesia.

That is not all. In fact, fresh resurgence of Hinduism is sweeping through Indonesia in modern times. In the early 1970's, the Toraja people of Sulawesi were the first to be identified under the umbrella of Hinduism. This was followed by Karo Batak of Sumatra in 1977 and the Ngaju Dayak of Kalimantan in 1980. Many recent converts to Hinduism had been members of Sukarno's PNI who now support his daughter significantly named Megawati Sukarnoputri.

The new Hindu communities in Java tend to be concentrated around recently built temples or near archeological temple sites which are being reclaimed as places of Hindu worship. An important neo Hindu temple in eastern Java is located on the slope of Mount Semeru, Java's highest mountain. Mass conversion to Hinduism has taken place in the region around the Loka Moksha Jayabaya temple where the ancient Hindu King and Prophet Jayabaya is said to have achieved spiritual liberation (Moksha). Another such site is the new temple at Pucak Raung in East Java which is mentioned in Balinese literature as the place from where *Maharishi Markandaya* took Hinduism to Bali.

The spread of Hinduism in ancient times was not confined to Sri Lanka and Indonesia. It had extended to as far as Malaya and Thailand in South East Asia. The Vedic seer Agastya legends covered not only the whole India from extreme north to deep south but also the lands beyond the frontiers of India. The sites of Agastya's 'ashrams' have been located in many places right from the Himalayas to Kanya Kumari in India and the Malaya mountains in South East Asia. That is an evidence of spread of Hinduism in the Malaya peninsula right from the Vedic or epic periods. It also explains sizeable Hindu presence in present day Malayasia which is coming on since ancient times.

To sum up, the spread of Hinduism extended across the southern sea to the Islands of the archipelago, Thailand and Indochina in South East Asia. So much so that at some time or the other in the past, Hindu kingdoms came to be established in south East Asian countries like, Vietnam, Cambodia, Thailand etc. Hindu symbols and ceremonies are still in vogue in Thailand. Ganga is still revered as a sacred river by the Thai people who make it a point to collect Ganga water when ever on a visit to India. In fact Ganga water is religiously used to sanctity the coronation of a Thai king or prince.

That was the range and sweep of Hinduism or Hindu civilization right from its beginning in India. The remarkable fact about its wide spread in South East Asia was that it was not the result of any conquest or imposition by the might of the sword. Hinduism has never been a proselytizing religion like Christianity and Islam. It was the marvelous spiritual force of Hinduism which led to its expansion beyond the borders of India. And it is this basic spirituality of Hindu civilization which has sustained and kept it alive for thousands of years while other ancient civilizations have long been consigned to history. Based on the new chronology of Rigvedic age, which makes it around 6000 years old, India the home of Hindu civilization, may well be regarded as "the cradle of civilization."

6

The Buddhist Interlude

For thousands of years beginning the Rigvedic period, Hinduism continued to have full sway not only over the whole of the Indian sub-continent but also large parts of south East Asia. It remained intact undisturbed by any other faith or philosophy till as late as around 500 years before Christ in its diverse manifestations. The 'Sanatan Dharma' (eternal religion) as defined by Sri Aurobindo, referred to earlier, has ever been so universalist and inclusive that it flourished for millennia embracing such diverse cults as Vaishnavism, Shaivism and Shaktyism as parts of mainstream Hinduism. "The large and old Hindu civilization," in the words of Klansk Klostermaier, "quietly appropriated whatever was brought into it from the outside, absorbed it, transformed it and made it part of its own." (A short History of Hinduism, Klaus K. Klostermaier, 2005).

This holistic Hindu tradition was apparently confronted for the first time at the beginning of the 5th century B.C. by a prince turned seer who came to be known as the 'Buddha,' the enlightened one. The community or creed of yellow-robed followers that he founded and his teachings had tremendous impact on the placid current of Hindu civilization. So much so that A.L. Bashan describes him as "The greatest man to have been born in India." (The wonder that was India, A.L. Bashan, 1981.) More about it later, but first a brief account of the prince turned the Buddha.

He was the son of King Suddhodhana, the chief of Sakya tribe of Nepal Terai. Like in the case of other sages and seers of ancient times, there are legends about his birth. One night queen Mahamya, his mother, had a strange dream about being bathed in a divine lake in the Himalayas and approached by a white elephant with a lotus flower. It was interpreted by the pundits of the court to indicate that she has conceived a greet son who would be either a 'universal emperor' or a 'Universal Teacher'. She gave birth to this wonderful child at Lumbini near Kapilvastu, the capital of the Sakyas. He was given the name Siddhartha, even as his 'gotra' name or family title was Gautam. His father wanted to make him 'universal emperor, rather than the 'Universal Teacher'. To that end, he resolved not to allow his son to know the miseries of the world. He was brought up in the beautiful ambience of the royal splendour, shielding him from all traces of sorrows of the world, wretchedness, disease and death. But god or destiny had willed otherwise.

One day while roaming about in his chariot, he saw an old man decripated by advancing age. He felt very unhappy when told by his charioteer that every one who was born in this world was bound to grow old like that. Next, he saw a very sick man severely afflicted with fever and ulcers in the last stage of his life. And then he saw a dead body being carried by his weeping kinsmen for cremation. Finally, he saw a wandering man in simple yellow robe evidently at complete peace with himself as a religious-beggar. That brought him instant relief. He had found his role model. He would give up his princely life and become a roving ascetic seeking liberation from the miseries of the world.

Siddhartha Gautam thus took to the life of a religious wanderer in search of the way to attain ultimate bliss. In the process, he learnt the mode of meditation, was taught the upanishadic view of the 'Brahman' or world soul by a vedic sage and went through rigorous penance for wearing out his 'Karma'. But he found no peace and kept moving from place to place until he reached the town of Gaya in the kingdom of Magadh. He sat underneath a large peepal tree on the out-skirts of the town determined not to leave his seat until he knew the truth about human suffering. On the 40th day of his deep meditation, he received enlightenment about the cause of human suffering and the way to get over it. Siddhartha Gautam thus became the fully enlightened one, the Buddha.

He preached his first sermon at the Dear park near Varanasi (the modern Sarnath) and gathered his first five disciples. This sermon was called the 'Turning of the wheel of Law' which became the nucleus of Buddhist teaching. It encapsuled the Four Noble Truths and the Eight-fold path which came to be the core of Buddhism. The Four Noble Truths are - (1) the world is full of suffering, (2) suffering is caused by human desires, (3) renunciation of desire is the path to salvation, and (4) salvation is possible through the Eight Fold Path, also termed as the Middle Path. It comprises eight principles of action such as 'right views', 'right resolve', 'right conduct' , 'right livelihood', 'right meditation' etc. Freedom from suffering, that is salvation, lay in freedom from the wheel of re-birth leading to 'nirvana' or extinction.

In other words, Buddhism holds that the cycle of birth, life, death and re-birth is the source of all suffering. The cycle is kept going by desires or cravings of human beings. Once man conquers his thirst or craving, he would secure release from the chain of re-births and consequential sorrow and suffering. That is the stage of 'nirvana', a calmy state of complete extinction.

Gautam Buddha's magnificient personality dazzled the religious scene in India. His teachings, which initially did not require much abstract thinking, had an instant appeal for the people. Because he discarded abstract philosophy, elaborate rituals and animal sacrifices associated with the old vedic practices. He used the common language of the area in which he lived which was 'Prakrit'. It was 'Prakrit' from which the 'Pali' language developed in which all early Buddhist scriptures were written. Above all, Buddhism rejected the caste hierarchy, specially the supremacy of the Brahmins, and threw its door open for all, bringing the high and low on the same spiritual platform. As a result, Buddhism fast became popular among the classes as well as the masses.

Starting with the Magadh region, it gradually spread in the northern and western parts of the country winning over the rulers and the ruled in its sweep. Ashoka and Kanishka, the Emperors of India, came within its fold, which made it the royal religion. This gave a fillip to the spread of Buddhism beyond the borders of India. Kind Deva nampia Tissa of Sri Lanka embraced Buddhism in Ashoka's time and it started becoming an international religion. In course of time, it spread far and wide from Afghanistan in the west to Japan in the East and Tibet and parts of China in the North. Apart from its popular appeal and easy accessibility, Buddhism was propagated by an order ('Sangha') of Yellow-robed monks which was perhaps the first highly disciplined monastic order in the world. That largely accounts for its expansion in India and large parts of East Asia.

But with all its dazzling success, Buddhism was no more than an out-growth of the all pervasive Hindu civilisation. In fact, it was very much a part of the great Hindu family of religious faiths. It was rooted in the doctrine of 'Karma' enshrined in the upanishads. Its concept of 'nirvana' as the ultimate panacea against wordly by sorrows and sufferings also emanated from the upanishadic philosophies. It flourished in India for a long time, not really as a separate religion altogether but as a heterodox sect of Hinduism into which it ultimately got absorbed. More of it in the next chapter.

7

The Hindu Assimilation

The Hindus too viewed Buddhism more or less the same way. So much so that long after Buddha's departure, he came to be regarded by Hindus in medieval India as the 9th of the ten avatars (incarnations) of the great God Vishnu himself. Jaideva, the famous devotional poet, observed in his, 'Geet Gobind' that Vishnu Became Buddha out of compassion for animals to put an end to the practice of animal sacrifice.

All that would go to show that Buddhism did not really emerge as an altogether separate religion In India in the garb of a rival or antagonistic to Hinduism. Nor probably Gautam Buddha intended it to be so. It came up and developed only as a heterodox sect of Hinduism, albeit a very powerful and distinct one. In the circumstances, there was nothing so surprising if it was eventually absorbed by the all pervasive Hindu civilization with its marvelous power of assimilation. So much so that until recent times, the Buddha temple at Bodh Gaya was in the hands of Hindu priests where the deity was worshipped by Hindus as well as Buddhist pilgrims from foreign lands.

At best, Buddhism and another contemporaneous heterodox sect Jainism can be regarded as protest movements against caste hierarchy that had gripped the Hindu society at that time. Both, Gautam Buddha and Vardhaman Mahavira, the founders of Buddhism and Jainism, were basically Hindu reformers. Both came from royal kshatriya stock out to challenge the monopoly of Brahmins in the religious sphere. Both sought to reform Hinduism by discarding animal sacrifice and Brahmin domination, but not to destroy it. Their followers were not required to give up their deep rooted belief in traditional Hindu Gods who continued to be venerated by both Buddhists and Jains. The continuity of the ancient Hindu civilization was thus not broken by the rise of Buddhism and Jainism as reform movements against caste hierarchy.

In any case, it is absolutely incorrect to regard caste system as an essential part of Hinduism. The system or order of four 'Varnas' or castes was basically an occupational arrangement that developed in Hindu society in ordinary course. The system did not exist in 'rig vedic' times, even though the moral and intellectual superiority of Brahmins can be traced to the practice of sacrificial rites. For, performance of these rites needed a priestly class to guide it. This led to the pre-eminence of the Brahmins who jealously guarded their ceremonial purity and exclusiveness.

But it is utterly wrong, even mischievous, to dub Hinduism as Brahmanism as many western and some motivated Indian historians have done. Voices against caste distinctions and inequality have been raised not only by Hindu reformers of modern and medieval times but also by those of ancient times. For Instance, in Mahabharata, Bharadwaja tells Bhrigu, *"we all seem to be affected by desire, anger, fear, sorrow, worry, hunger, and labour; how do we have caste differences then?"* Further, in 'Bhavisya Purana' it is observed that all castes are children of God and they all belong to the same caste. "All human beings have the same father, and children of the same father cannot have different castes." (Quoted in 'The Argumentative Indian' By Amartya Sen, 2005.)

In this sense, protest against caste distinctions represented by Buddhism and Jainism was also not outside the ancient Hindu tradition. In fact, it was very much a part of it, which found expression much later in the Hindu Bhakti movement of the Middle Ages and preaching of Swami Vivekananda and Dayanand Saraswati in modern times.

With the royal patronage of Emperors like Ashoka and Kanishka and missionary Zeal of Buddhist monks (the "Sangha"), Buddhism had a phenomenal growth during the First thousand years of its birth. Apart from large parts of India (northern and western) and Afghanistan, it held sway over South East Asia and the Far East. From Sri Lanka, which turned Buddhist in Ashoka's time, it was taken to Burma, Vietnam, Thailand, Cambodia, etc. Another branch of Buddhism (the Great Wheel) was taken to China and thence to Japan by a succession of Buddhist monks. During all this period, India was looked upon by the East Asians as a Buddhist country.

Buddhism in some form or the other survived as a recognizable religion in such diverse countries of Asia as China, Japan, Korea, Vietnam and Cambodia. It co-existed with Confucianism in China, Shintoism in Japan and other local sects in the South East Asian countries. In this background, scholars and historians are puzzled why Buddhism did not survive as a dominant religion in India, the land of its origin. Those who attribute this apparent paradox to such superficial factors as the decline of the Buddhist Mauryas and their supercession by the Guptas who did not subscribe to Buddhism, miss the basic point.

The issue itself, that is the question of non-existence of Buddhism as a parallel dominant religion in India, is irrelevant in the first place. It is based on misconception or outright ignorance of the umbrella character of Hinduism or the Hindu civilization.

For Buddhism itself was rooted in the philosophic tradition of basic Hindu scriptures like the Upanishads. The Upanishadic theory of 'Karma' affecting and regulating future births is the core of Buddhism. According to it, 'dukkha', that is the cycle of re-birth and death is kept going by the thirst ('tanha') or craving of the individual. If this craving or desire for anything is given up and man accepts the inevitable end of all phenomenal things, the ultimate state of calm is reached. It is indestructible. It is 'nirvana', that is extinction or end of re-birth. In other words, human desires which lead to 'karma' are the cause of all sorrows and sufferings. But this is in essence what some of the main Upanishads say. 'Kena Upanishad', which forms part of Upanishad Brahmana of Samaveda, holds that our only duty is to renounce all desires in order to attain the desirable world that is "birthless, undecaying, immortal, fearless". It says that in the case of one who cherishes desires, even the rites enjoined in the Vedas become the cause of return to the world, that is re-birth. Accordingly, only a desireless man of pure mind who has renounced all transitory external things aspires for knowledge of the indwelling self. And in the Mundaka Upanishad of Atharveda, it is said that only a man of detachment who resorts to renunciation can realize the knowledge of in-dwelling self. The realization of this in-dwelling self ('atman') as 'Brahman' or Supreme soul removes all ignorance which is the cause of desire and 'karma'.

It is thus evident that the Buddhist ideal of desirelessness as the key to avoidance of re-birth and achieving salvation was basically Upanishadic. Being not very distinct from the parent religion of Hinduism, Buddhism sought to emerge as some sort of a super doctrine to lead its followers on the path of salvation discarding the Vedic sacrificial rites. It also abandoned the

Upanishadic view that knowledge of the indwelling self and its one-ness with the world soul was the key to salvation. Instead, it preached the Eight-Fold path of right conduct and right meditation. But in this also, it was influenced by the older Hindu system of 'yoga' and 'dhyana'. The Hindu philosophies of 'Sankhya' and 'Nyaya' had their marked imprint on Buddhism as it developed in course of its evolution and growth. No wonder that scholars like A.J. Basham have described Buddhism as one of the heterodox sects of Hinduism.

In any case, what Dr. Vincent Smith calls popular Buddhism as practiced by the commoners was not the same as the rigorous teaching of the scriptures followed and preached by Boudh Bhiksus (monks). It included many practices and beliefs of old Hinduism. Even though it denied the authority of the Vedas, popular Buddhism did not interfere with the time-honoured belief in Hindu Gods. Many of its followers continued to avail of the services of Hindu priests on occasions like births, marriages and deaths. By the time of the Gupta period, Buddhist monks often participated in Hindu processions. For the lay Buddhist, his faith was one among other prevallent cults which all led to salvation and commanded veneration.

8

A Shining Star in The South

Although Buddhism never developed as a rival religion challenging the broad parameters of Hinduism, it did have sway over wide areas in India for more than a thousand years as a strong heterodox sect. With royal patronage from powerful emperors like Ashoka and Kanishka and its wide spread in South and East Asia - Sri Lanka, Japan and China - it developed an over-size image as a distinct religion in the world at large. But in India, whatever remained of Buddhism even as a heterodox sect was eventually polished off by the renewed surge of intellectual Hinduism. It was a surge which not only marginalized Buddhism in India but also galvanized a new look Hinduism to occupy centre-stage in the country. And it emanated not from the so-called Aryan North but from the Dravidland of the South. (That incidentally underlines the essential oneness of Hinduism which has always encompassed the whole of India).

The progenitor of this resurgent Hinduism was a bright star appearing in the Southern sky and dazzling the whole Country like a meteor-Adi Shankaracharya. Through his elaborate commentaries on principal Upanishads, extensive travels across the country, engaging in brilliant arguments with Buddhists and others, and founding of an order of Hindu monks, Adi Shankaracharya not only ended the sway of Buddhism in India but more. He raised philosophical Hinduism to a new high by developing the doctrines of Vedanta based on the Upanishads. He revived or renewed the pristine glory of Hinduism which enabled it to withstand the onslaught of aggressive Islamism knocking at India's door, the full blast of which was only a few centuries away.

The Vedanta school of Hindu or Indian philosophy is a formulation derived from volumes of spiritual observations of sages and seers who had searched for the ultimate truth. Adi Shankaracharya gave a consistent philosophical shape to the statements of the Upanishadic sages in his doctrine of Vedanta which has come to be the identifying mark of Hindu civilization. It has had such eminent followers as Swami Vivekananda, Sri Aurobindo and Dr. Radhakrishnan in modern India. It is still a living school of Hindu philosophical thought subscribed to by numerous theologicians and Hindu intellectuals.

Before dwelling upon his Vedantist doctrines, a brief account of Shankara's life and times would be appropriate. As usual in case of such sages and seers of the past, his life story which tradition has preserved for us is partly in legend and partly in written documents. In absence of any authentic biography, there is no unanimity among scholars about his exact date of birth and span of life.

One of his biographers, Anandagiri, takes his date of birth back to the pre-Christian era, holding that he was born in the year 44 B.C. (Before Christ) and died at the age of 32 in the year 12 B.C. But this view is not supported by other scholars, almost all of whom place him between 8th and 9th Centuries AD. Here also, one writer Venkiteshwara holds that Shankaracharya lived for 92 years from 805 AD to 897 AD, on the ground that he could not have achieved so mLch as he did in the short life span of 32 years. This view too is not shared by anyone else, the near unanimous opinion among scholars being that Shankaracharya lived for 32 years only. That he did so much to rejuvenate Hinduism and place it on such a high pedestal in such a short life span is a true measure of his brilliance, greatness and godliness. The generally accepted view held by Max Muller, MacDonnell, Dr. Radhakrishnan and others is that he was born in 788 A.D. and died at the age of 32 in 820 A.D.

There is no such dispute, however, about his parentage and place of birth. By all accounts, Shankaracharya was born in a village near Kaladi in the erstwhile Cochin state, now a part of Kerala, in a family of Namboodiri Brahmins. His father Shivguru and mother Aryamba were devotees of Lord Shiva. When they remained childless for a long time, they invoked the grace of Lord Shiva to bless them with a child. Legend has it that one night God Shiva himself appeared in Aryamba's dream and asked her to choose either a long living dunce or a short-lived genius as a son. She opted for the genius. Anlandaagiri records that God Shiva, who was eager to be born on earth to rejuvenate the declining Vedic tradition, himself entered Aryamba's womb to be born as Shankara.

Having lost his father at the age of seven, Shankara showed amazing talent as a young student at his family teacher's home. He is said to have mastered the Vedas within a year and returned to his mother. She wanted him to marry and settle down to a family life, but this was not to be. She was reminded by a sage that the boy was to die young, being the wise but short-lived child she had opted for in her dream. Even as a very young boy, Shankara started developing a keen desire to take to a life of asceticism. With great difficulty, he was able to make his mother agree to his going in for an ascetic's life.

Accordingly, Shankara left home in search of a teacher who could initiate him into the holy order of "Sanyasa" (asceticism). That led him to a great "Sanyasi", Gobind Bhagwatpada, based on the banks of river Narmada. It was under him that Shankara got his first lessons as a "Sanyasi". His Guru Gobinda was himself a disciple of Guru Gandapada, one of the early writers of commentaries on "Brahma-Sutra" or "Vedanta Sutra" which form the basic text of Vedanta philosophy. It is said that the temple at Badari was subsequently built to commemorate Shankara's initiation into "Sanyas" at that place.

After completing his course of instruction, Shankara became a peripatetic or roving teacher of religion in course of which he arrived at Varanasi. With his extra-ordinary intellect and mastery of the religious texts, he soon made his mark among the theologians and philosophers based at Varanasi and attracted a number of pupils. It was here that he spent some years writing or starting to write various commentaries on scriptural texts for which he is famous. These included his well-known commentary on "Brahma Sutra" followed by commentaries on the ten leading Upanishads.

At Varanasi, Shankara also acted as a great reformer against spiritual chaos and degeneration. Religion at this point of time had sunk into mere rituals and sacrifices. The followers of Buddha had reduced their philosophy to empty nothingness and monasteries had become breeding places of quack philosophers. Diverse sects indulging in meaningless rituals and ceremonies were engaged in senseless polemics with each other. Shankara disputed with them vigorously and swept them off with his sharp intellectual campaign against irrationality and ignorance.

As regards Shankara's inter-face with Buddhist heterodoxy, Swami Vivekananda writes: "Shankara came as a great philosopher and showed that the real essence of Buddhism and that of the Vedanta are not very different, but that the disciples did not understand the master and have degraded themselves, denied the existence of the Soul and of God and have become atheists. That was what Shankara showed and all the Buddhists began to come back to the old religion".

But in his reforming zeal, Shankara did not ride roughshod with the prevailing faith of the common people. As Hindus then worshipped one or the other of five gods - Sun, Shakti, Vishnu, Shiva and Ganapati - Shankara guided them to worship the gods as an aid to their spiritual growth. For he showed that as man can only travel slowly on the upward road, all the varied presentations were needed to suit his varying capacity. Shankara thus laid the foundation of unity among diverse sects which has sustained Hinduism right up to this day.

9

Adi Shankaracharya; The Roving Saint-Philosopher, who Revitalized Hinduism

After his reforming work at Varanasi, Shankara left on a countrywide tour to carry on with his mission of religious reform and spiritual enlightenment. His first stop was at Prayag (Allahabad) which was the base of Kumaril Bhatta, the famous champion of "Purva Mimansa" school of Vedic theology. It was rooted in the belief that performance of sacrifices was the means to attain everything, which Shankara disputed. But there is no record of his confronting any follower of "Purva Mimansa" at Prayag, from where he moved on to Mahishamati.

It was here that he met the well-known "Mimansaka" Mandan Mishra belonging to that doctrinal school. Mandan; Mishra was the Chief Pundit at the Court of Mahishamati leading a life of luxury. Shankara entered into a full-fledged disputation with Mandan Mishra which lasted for 17 days. Bharati, the scholarly wife of Mandan, acted as the umpire at the heated debate (Bharati was believed to be the incarnation of Saraswati, the goddess of learning). At the end of it, Mandan was roundly defeated and joined the ascetic order as a follower of Shankara.

This was followed by Shankara's second great debate with Bharati herself which too lasted for another 17 days. There are legends about Bharatt, finding him un-beatable, challenging Shankara to a discussion on "Kama Shastra" and how he managed to defeat her in that also. Thereafter, Bharati is said to have followed him along with Mandana to his new destination in the South.

His next stop was at a place on the banks of river Tungabhadra now famous as Sringeri. It was here that he established the first of the four main 'Pesthas' or religious seminaries which Shankara set up in the four corners of the Country. He made Mandana Mishra, now his disciple, the head of the seminary and also got a temple built in the memory of Bharati. The temple is still there, dedicated to the goddess of learning whom Bharati was believed to represent.

There was a brief interlude in Shankara's tireless travels when he visited his village home on his mother's death. After performing her last rites as a dutiful son, he returned to Sringeri, collected his pupils and proceeded on his all India tour. In course of his journey, he stayed at Puri in Orissa for some time. He set up the second of his seminaries known as Gobardan Peetha which has flourished down to this day.

After Puri, he appears to have moved westwards stopping at Ujjain. There he confronted a fanatic sect known as "Bhairvas" who believed in human sacrifice. He overcame and wiped them out through learned discourses and disputations. Proceeding further west, he toured Gujarat Desha (modern Gujarat State) and established his third seminary or Peetha at Dwaraka.

Thereafter Shankara moved northwards traveling as far as Kashmir, vanishing his challengers and critics on the way.

Kashmir then was Buddhist, full of vain and hollow theoreticians whom he challenged and defeated in arguments. So much so that he ascended the seat of learning in the capital of Kashmir. It is still famous today as Shankaracharya hill on the outskirts of Srinagar.

He then came down to the plains of north India and proceeded eastwards following the course of river Ganga. Traveling through Bengal, he went as far as Guwahati in Assam. That was virtually the last phase of his relentless travels; which dazzled the country. On his return journey from Assam, he went on to Badri in the north where he built a temple of God Narain (Vishnu). He also established a Seminary at Joshi Math, the fourth and the last of the series of Hindu "Peetha" set up by him in the country.

Having achieved his mission of rejuvenating Hinduism through the length and breadth of India, Shankara, now known as Adi Shankaracharya, retired to Kedarnath beyond Badri. It was here that he entered into a cave to achieve "Samadhi" at the young age of 32 years and did not return.

Shankara's long journeys throughout this vast land at a time when travel was so difficult with hardly any means of transport worth the name speaks volumes about his mission. It was a sacred mission of uniting the whole Country through the common thread of universalist Hindu philosophy of Vedanta arising out of the Upanishads. He developed and propagated the philosophy of "Advaita" or non-dualist Vedanta elaborated in his twelve monumental commentaries, especially, the commentary on "Vedanta Shutras'. His Advaita philosophy represerts the essential unity of Hinduism and Hindu or Indian philosophical thought right upto this day. He defined and dwelt upon the current catchwords like "Maya" and "Karma" and left the terminology of Hinduism as it is today.

The core of Shankaracharya's teaching is the essential oneness of "Atma" or pure innermost self with "Brahman" or the ultimate reality perceived as godhead. When an individual overcomes 'avidya' or ignorance, and realizes the unity between the "Atman" (innermost self) and "Brahman" (the ultimate reality) he becomes a liberated soul, waiting only for his final liberation from the body by death. The liberated self or "Atman", is in the nature of pure consciousness and pure bliss. The material universe or the world is merely an external phenomenon which functions on the basis of the law of "Karma", but its ultimate cause is "Brahman" which has created it. Since "Brahman" is the only ultimate Reality and cause of all things, all creation is nothing but "Maya" or the power of illusion. The world exists within the realm of "Maya" superimposed by "Brahman" like the mirage lake seen in a desert.

But to hold that "Brahman" is real and the universe an illusion does not mean a denial of the world in the life of man. Shankara's philosophy does not discourage man from performing his wordly duties faithfully and cheerfully. It only holds that the individual soul manifests the Supreme "Brahman" in its love for the body, for the family, for the nation and for the entire humanity. It is a thing to be practiced, a way of life, a means for coming to terms with life, its joys and sorrows. For once a man gets rid of "avidya" (ignorance) and realizes that he is one with the ultimate Reality ('Aham Brahman'), he gives up his ego, which is the repository of all miseries and petty pleasures. It is like losing our ego-hood in deep sleep, in the enjoyment of great art, in loving our beloved ones, which make life worth living.

Thus, Shankara's philosophy is not a mere abstraction. It is a way of life. Once we realize that our miseries and fears arise out of wrongly identifying ourselves with the phenomenal world which is "Maya" or illusion, we can fruitfully strive for "Sat Chit Anandam"- absolute existence, absolute consciousness and absolute bliss. The inner self is not to be identified with the body of man which is perishable, but with consciousness which is indestructible and eternal.

Far from being a philosophy of negation, Shankara's Vedanta had a very positive message for mankind in the background of the prevailing message of Buddhism. Sorrow and suffering were the startling point of Buddhism. There is no end to the pain of old age, disease and death because man will be reborn. The remedy according to the philosophy of Buddhism is "Nirvana" or total extinction. This was a totally negative concept implying double tragedy-suffering ended by complete extinction. It was like "the sleep of the dreamless man who never wakes up". (Nirad C. Chowduri in his book *The Continent of Circe*, 1965).

Shankara's Vedanta converted this "Nirvana" into the positive concept of "Mokshya" or Salvation. "Mokshya" is to be found by regarding the external world which is changeable and destructible as "Maya" or illusion and identifying with the "Brahman" or ultimate soul which is infinite and eternal. It is in this union of the individual soul with the ultimate Reality or Supreme Soul that there is indestructible joy or absolute bliss. Thus while denying the reality of wordly pleasures, Shankara put another kind of eternal joy before mankind, avoiding the double tragedy implicit in total extinction or "Nirvana".

Adi Shankaracharya thus not only wiped out the negative fall-out of life-denial implicit in the Buddhist philosophy, but also put a new life into the "Sanatan Dharma" that is Hinduism. More of it in the next chapter.

10

Adi Shankaracharya - The Saviour of Hindu Identity

With all the heights and subtleties of his Vedanta Philosophy, Shankara did not propound any new doctrine outside the parameters of the ancient Vedic religion. His philosophy was at best an exposition or codification of the observations of Upanishadic sages. And principal or main Upanishads are very much a part of the Vedas. The term "Vedanta" literally means the end of the Vedas, which actually refers to the main Upanishads. Because Upanishads are not only the end portions of the Vedas but also their goal, culmination or end.

Shankara regarded Hindu scriptures as of eternal value, not because a personal God wrote them, but because they contained incontrovertible truth. They contained the fruits of practical religious experiments and spiritual insights of several sages and seers who had searched for the ultimate truth. Shankara's philosophy of Advaita "(non-dualism)" that is the integral oneness of "Atma" with "Brahman", was therefore an elaboration of the Hindu scriptures and not a substitute for them.

Shankara knew that the ordinary man could not comprehend the height of his philosophy of non-dualism (Advaita) in one go. He therefore made a distinction between "lower" and "higher" knowledge to lead the common man step by step to the realization of Advaiata" or unity with "Brahman". The portions of the Vedas which laid down rituals and prayers were regarded by him as lower knowledge to guide ordinary humans away from their sensual lives. The lower knowledge is the essential first step similar to the over-simplified pictures with the help of which a child is taught. Just as childhood is not despised, lower knowledge is not to be berated.

On the other hand, the Upanishads contained the higher knowledge meant for those who had renounced carnal desires and attained some measure of enlightenment. But everyone wanting to reach the heights of enlightenment has to start at the bottom to move up step by step from lower to higher knowledge. Shankara's Vedanta was thus a continuation and reinforcement of the Vedic religion that is Hinduism.

Apart from providing a solid philosophic and spiritual base to the ancient Hindu Civilization, he also did his bit to give it a lasting organizational or institutional shape. He did it by establishing four *"Peethas"* or Hindu religious seminaries in the four corners of the Country at Sringeri in the south, Puri in the east, Dwaraka in the West and Joshi Math near Badrinath in the North. These "Peethas" are still the standard -bearers of Hinduism in India, presided over by their respective heads known as Shankaracharyas.

Adi Shankaracharya thus laid the foundation of organized Hinduism by providing it with an institutional framework for the first time in its long history. In this respect, he can justifiably be regarded as the greatest seer and apostle of Hinduism after the Vedic and epic periods, that is, of historical Hinduism.

He proved to be the bulwark against the most serious assault on Hinduism or Hindu Civilization which was in the offing. That was the tornado of Islamism or politico-religious phenomenon of Islam which was sweeping across West Asia, North Africa, South East Europe and knocking at India's door.

In fact, Islamism had already arrived in India on its Western fringe by the time Adi Shankaracharya appeared on the scene and galvanized Hinduism in the rest of the Country. That is, if the popularly held view is accepted that he was born in 788 AD. For Mahammad-bin-Qasim had attacked Sindh with the blessings of the Caliph in the year 712 AD and conquered it. The Hindus and Buddhists were given the option of embracing Islam or facing death. A great massacre went on for three days in which all adults who refused to embrace Islam were put to death. But, that was only a relatively minor pointer to the shape of things to come which the rest of the Country did not take note of.

The more brutal onslaught of Islamism came three and half centuries later when Mahmud Ghazni entered India "Sword in hand" with the twin objective of spreading Islam and plundering the Country. The most savage of his assaults on Hinduism was the sacking and destruction of the famous Somnath temple in Gujarat in the 11th century. But the real founder of Muslim Empire in India was Muhammad Ghori who defeated the legendry Hindu ruler of Delhi Prithvi Raj Chauhan towards the end of the 12th century. Since then rulers changed, dynasties changed until the famed Mughals came over to establish a more organized Islamic rule over India in the first half of the 16th century. The absolutist Mughal rule lasted till the end of Aurangzeb in the year 1707.

India thus remained under unadulterated Muslim rule for well over 500 years. And all Muslim rulers, with the solitary exception of Akbar, did every thing to Islamise the country, as

Islamic conquerors had done in Egypt, Mesopotamia, Persia and Afghanistan. And yet, the wonder that is Hindu Civilization withstood the challenge and India could not be Islamised as the other ancient civilizations referred to above had been. Apart from the innate spiritual strength of the shock-absorbing Vedic religion that is Hinduism, Adi Shankaracharya played a stellar role in preserving and keeping it intact.

He did it in two ways. First, he re-invigorated Hinduism through his extensive travels across the country, uniting different sects and focused upon the basics of the Upanishadic religion represented in his philosophy of Vedanta. At the same time, he provided an institutional base to Hinduism by establishing some sort of a monastic order in the shape of four "Peethas" or Seminaries at Sringeri, Puri, Dwaraka and Joshi Math.

The second, and perhaps more important contribution of Adi Shankaracharya in preventing the Islamization of India was indirect. His reinforced Hinduism absorbed and ended the sway of Buddhism as a separate religion, which was doomed to become the softest target of Islamists. A.L. Basham writes :Hinduism ... .suffered from the Muslim invasion but was not severely weakened by it. Buddhism could not stand up to the change. In the first rush of the Muslim advance down the Ganga, Nalanda and other great monasteries of Bihar were sacked, libraries were burnt and monks were put to the sword. (*The Wonder that was India,* by A.L. Basham).

With its focus on world renunciation and ultimate extinction ("Nirvana"), Buddhism was the easiest prey of aggressive Islamism and was wiped out by it in India. Kashmir which was predominantly Buddhist became predominantly Muslim in course of the Muslim rule. Afghanistan which had come under the sway of Ashoka's Empire and turned Buddhist was completely Islamized in course of the first flush of the Arab

Islamic conquest of the Middle East. Sri Lanka, Burma, Tibet and Ladakh remained Buddhist because they did not come under Muslim rule.

In such a backdrop, it can safely be concluded that if India had become predominantly Buddhist before the arrival of the Islamists, it would have been as thoroughly Islamized during the long Muslim rule as Kashmir and Afghanistan. To the extent that Adi Shankaracharya checkmated Buddhism through resurgent Hinduism, and prevented India from turning predominantly Buddhist, he made a singular contribution in preserving the Hindu identity of India inspite of over 500 years of Muslim rule. In this respect, he can be considered as the greatest savior of the great Hindu civilization through the most severe challenge faced by it in course of its long history.

11

The Dark Ages

In the Western World, the period between the end of the ancient Greeko-Roman civilization and the beginning of the modern age is termed as the "Middle Age". Scholars and humanists of European "Renaissance" who started glorifying the classical civilization of ancient Greece and Rome dubbed this period as "dark". In their excessive appreciation of the beauties of their ancient civilization, which had been nearly eclipsed by the ascendancy of the Church during the Middle Ages, they tended to denounce or berate this period as "Dark Ages". This description was only figurative or metaphorical in case of Europe. In case of India, however, the medieval age turned out to be a "dark" age in a more literal sense.

In broad terms, going by the religion of the outsiders who came to rule over the Country, the medieval age is known as the Muslim period in Indian history. That in itself does not make it 'dark'. For at different times in the past also, outsiders like the Shakas, Kushans and Huns had come to rule over large parts of India. But in course of time, the inclusive Hindu civilization aborted or assimilated them all, making them integral part of Indian identity. For instance, Wema Kah Phises, the second Kushan King of India, was a worshipper of Lord Shiva whose image he got engraved on his coins. And Kanishka, the most famous Kushan King of India, was a great patron of Budhism. In fact, the last great Kushan King, Vasudeva I, who ruled from 152 to 176 AD, was a Hindu, and a worshipper of God Shiva whose image is found in most of his coins. The Huns, who were a great warrior tribe, got absorbed into the Rajput population of India.

But not so in case of the Arab, Afgan and Turko-Afgan Muslims who came to rule over India during the medieval times. They came 'sword in hand' with the avowed objective of spread of Islam and destruction or elimination of the indigenous Hindu Civilization. Here a distinction must be made between Islam as a pure religious faith or mode of worship and Islamism as a politico-religious ideology out to conquer the world. Initially, Islam as a pure religious faith came to India with the Arab Muslims who visited the Coastal areas in the South and West in ordinary course. They travelled to these parts of India, built their mosques, preached their religion and sometimes even converted people, like the Christians earlier and later. Hinduism took it in its stride and interacted with Islam on a purely religious plank. It made no difference to the universalist and tolerant Hindu civilization.

But political Islam or Islamism as an extremely intolerant and conquering phenomenon was a different proposition altogether. When it entered India with "fire and slaughther" in the shape of Mahmud Ghazni's invasions beginning the year 1000 AD, it hit the Hindu civilization like a tornado. Mahamud of Gazni was conferred the title of Amin-ul-Millat (Custodian of the Faith) by the reigning Caliph of Islam-Al-Quadir Billah - and asked to lead expeditions against India year after year. Accordingly, he raided India 17 times beginning the year 1000 until his death in 1030. Among his more brutal assaults were at Peshawar where 15,000 Hindus were killed, at Mahawan in Mathura district where 50,000 Hindus were massacred and drowned in river Jamna, at Mathura and Brindaban where all temples and idols of Lord Krishna were destroyed and at Kannauj where 10,000 Hindu temples were demolished. His most savage attack was at Somnath in Gujarat where the most venerated idol of Lord Somnath was destroyed and around 50,000 Hindu devotees who had gathered in the temple were butchered. Mahmud's Court Historian Utbi regarded Ghaznavi expeditions to India as Jihad or holy war for the destruction of Hindus and spread of Islam.

This blood-spilling intrusion of Islamism in the 11th Century, as the Arab Muslim conquest of Sindh earlier in the 8th Century, was a prelude to the eventual establishment of Islamic rule over India. Another Afgan Chief - Shahabuddin Muhammed Ghori laid the foundation of long lasting Muslim Empire in India after defeating Prithvi Raj Chauhan - the legendry King of Delhi - in the year 1192. Rulers changed, dynasties changed from Afgans to Turkish slaves to Mughals, but Islamists continued to rule over India until they were replaced by the British around the year 1757.

In West Asia, Mesopotamia, Egypt and Persia had been seats of thousands of years old civilizations in ancient times. But once they came under Muslim rule, Islam completely washed off their religious and civilizational past. Iraq, Syria (Mesopotamia), Iran (Persia) and Egypt have been so thoroughly Islamized that they have forgotten and written off their great ancient civilizations as of no consequence. In this back ground, it is a great wonder that inspite of well over 500 years of unadulterated Muslim rule, India did not turn into an Islamic nation like the above mentioned countries of West Asia. How come?

The answer lies in the strong spiritual roots of the abiding Hindu civilization which has enabled it to take any amount of assault in its stride and survive through the ages. In the 'dark' ages of Muslim rule when Islamism was at its aggressive peak, the innate, invincible spirituality of Hinduism got internalized in the minds and hearts of the tormented Hindu masses. This led to the birth of the 'bhakti' movement which enabled Hinduism to survive the most lethal assault on it in its long history of about 6000 years. The 'bhakti' movement was in essence the religion of the heart, kind of a totally devotional mode of worship focused on a particular God or deity. Everyone could worship the chosen God individually in their homes or collectively with others in common places of worship like temples. Hinduism was thus preserved in the minds and hearts of the vast majority of the Indian people inspite of every effort of Islamism to suppress and supercede it during the period of Muslim rule.

Here also, that great apostle and saviour of modern Hinduism - Adi Shankaracharya - contributed to the evolution of 'Bhaktism' in his own way. It is said that one day he got disgusted listening to a religious student at Varanasi learning Sanskrit grammar by rote. He spontaneously burst out into a devotional song: "worship Govinda, worship Govinda, worship Govinda, you fool! when you are face to face with death at the appointed time, grammatical formulae cannot save you". That in essence could be seen as an earlier manifestation of the 'Bhakti' movement which developed later as a great cushion or shield of Hinduism.

Shankar's philosophy of 'Advait' (non-dualism) or oneness of individual soul with the ultimate soul (Brahman) and dismissal of the world as 'Maya' or illusion also reinforced the 'Bhakti' movement indirectly. If the outer world was 'Maya' or illusion, so was the scourge of Islamism during Muslim rule. So why worry about it? Keep worshipping your God from the innermost recesses of your heart, which is 'bhakti' all about, shun all worldly threats and temptations and attain one-ness with the ultimate soul. Physical death would deliver you from the 'Maya' or illusion of the worldly existence and lead to "Mokshya" which is the state of eternal bliss. That was the message of Shankar's philosophy which nourished and sustained the "bhakti' movement, which in turn sustained Hinduism during its darkest period.

12

The Bhakti Movement

Conventional historians (Romilla Thapar, A.L. Basham Percival Spear etc.) have dwelt upon the so-called "Bhakti" movement as an altogether new cult that emerged in Hinduism in the Middle Ages. "The Bhakti movement, or religion, of the heart directed to a particular deity", writes Percival Spear, "spread from Western India among the Marathas into the Punjab where Guru Nanak (1469-1539) founded the sect later to be known as the Sikhs". (A History of India-2' by Percival Spear - 1968). This is an erroneous view based on imperfect understanding of the Vedic religion that is Hinduism. In fact, the origin of "Bhaktism" can be traced back to the Vedas themselves which continue to be the bed-rock of Hinduism right up to this day.

In fact, the 'Samhitas' or the main part of the Rigveda is nothing but a prayer book addressed to different gods like Indra, Varun, Rudra, Surya (Sun) and others. The prayers invoke the blessing of particular gods in terms which are so highly devotional as to be only a short step from 'Bhakti' of medieval Hindus. For instance, one of the hymns to God Varuna says :

"You are father, You are mother,
You are elder brother... .
You are gold, You are jewel, You are pearl-
You are lord, Rider on the Bull (Shiva), You are bliss,
Oh Bliss !O Light! I have taken refuge in You."

(English translation quoted in "The Wonder that was India" by A L Basham, 1967)

From such intensely devotional prayer to a personal God, 'Bhakti' towards a deity was only a short step forward. The Rigveda can thus be taken to be the fountain spring of devotional Hinduism which developed into a pervasive "Bhakti" movement during the "Dark Ages".

The worshippers of Vasudeva, identified with Vishnu and Krishna, known as "Bhagavatas" and those of Shiva known as "Pashupathas" can be considered as the predecessors of the medieval practitioners of "Bhakti". While the "Bhagwatas" flourished around a century before Christ, the "Pashupatas" came up a little later.

The Bhagawatas evidently drew inspiration from the "Bhagwadgita" of the later Vedic or Epic age which describes Arjun's devotional relationship with Krishna. Arjun regards Krishna's relationship with himself as that of father and son, friend and friend, lover and beloved, even though he is struck with awe and reverence when Krishna reveals himself as the God Supreme.

These ancient seedlings of "Bhakti" or devotional religion sprouted into the rich vegetation of full-fledged "Bhakti" movement during the Middle Ages when Hinduism came under massive assault of Islamism. Adi Shankaracharya had also given vent to his devotional instinct when he spontaneously composed the poems like "Bhajgovindam", even though he was primarily wedded to the Vedantic doctrine of "Adwait" (non-dualism) and salvation through knowledge of oneness with the Supreme Soul. It was a series of his successors who contributed to the growth and development of the "Bhakti" movement in their own way.

The earliest among them was Ramanujacharya who taught at the great seminary at Srirangam during the 11th and 12th centuries. (This was the period when temples were being destroyed, idols broken and Hindus massacred by the rapacious Islamist-Mahmud of Ghazni). Ramanuja pronounced that the best means of salvation was "Bhakti-Yoga", that is intense devotion to Vishnu in order to realize that the worshipper was only a fragment of God. The individual soul was one with God but was separate and achieved fulfillment in ultimate communion with Him. Accordingly Ramanuja's religious philosophy was known as "Vishist-advaita" or qualified non-dualism, but it was a step forward in the direction of full-fledged "Bhakti".

In his long life-span, said to be 120 years (1017 to 1137), Ramanujacharya traveled from Badrinath in the north to Rameshwaram in the South and Maharashtra in the West to Orissa in the east, preaching his religion of devotional worship of Vishnu the God. His real contribution was that he provided a solid philosophical base for the "Bhakti" movement to flourish in the days to come. It was thus logical for his line of disciples to carry forward the Bhakti movement to its full dimensions. One among them was Raghavacharya, but the most notable was Raghava's disciple Swamy Ramananda who spread the Bhakti movement in north India as well as Maharashtra in the West and Bengal and Assam in the east.

Like Adi Shankaracharya, Swamy Ramanand became an ascetic at the early age of 12 years and started studying the scriptures basing himself at Kashi (Varanasi). Hailed and supported by an army of disciples - saints and religious scholars-

Ramananda threw himself whole-heartedly in the spread of Bhakti movement in the country as a shield against the advance of Islamism during the 14th and 15th centuries. He shaped the Bhakti movement into a cushion against the aggressive onslaught of Islamism during the peak of Muslim rule in two ways.

First, he made Bhakti or devotional religion all inclusive, throwing its door open to men and women of all castes on the basis of perfect equality. Hindu society, it may be noted, was divided into castes, supposed to be high and low, which was being exploited by the Islamists to lure the so-called lower castes into Islam. His disciples in the fold of Bhakti included saint Kabir, a Julaha' or weaver, saint Sen, a barber, saint Raidas, a Chamar or Cobbler, saint Dhanna, a Jat, and numerous others belonging to diverse castes and classes-high and low, rich and poor. Thus the cult of Bhakti, as propounded by Swami Ramanand, promoted social equality in Hindu society, which prevented conversion to Islam in the name of social equality claimed to be its special attribute.

Not only that, Swami Ramanand started and gave sanctity to the process of bringing back into the Hindu fold those who had been forced or cajoled into Islam by dubious means. It was under his inspiration and initiative that thousands of those who had been forcibly converted into Islam in Ayodhya alone were reconverted into Hinduism and became Rambhaktas. This was a revolutionary step in the direction of Hindu revival at that time, which finds mention in "Bhavishya Puran".

His second most important contribution to the spread of Bhakti movement was the vernacularization of Bhakti literature. The earlier, Acharyas like Ramanujacharya, Madhavacharya and Raghavacharya had used only Sanskrit as the medium of their preachings. Deviating from that tradition, Swami Ramanand started writing in Hindi, the spoken language of north

India, so as to make Bhakti or devotional religion accessible to the common man. In the distant past, Gautam Buddha also had adopted Pali, the common language of the Magadha religion, as the medium of his religious discourse which made Buddhism a popular religion at that time. Swami Ramanand did just that for the Bhakti movement by coming down from the high pedestal of Sanskrit and taking recourse to the common language of the people to widen the sway of devotional Hinduism.

The vernacularisation of Bhakti literature initiated by him eventually resulted in a phenomenal growth of devotional poetry in local languages across the country. From Gujarat and Rajasthan in the West to Bengal and Assam in the East, the cult of Bhakti or religion of the heart spread among the Hindu masses, groaning under the pressure of Islamism, through the: poetic works of a succession of his line of disciples. Prominent among them were Goswami Tulsidas, Sant Kabir, Sant Raidas, Meerabai etc. In Maharashtra, the flag of Bhakti literature was carried forward by Sant Namdeo, Sant Gyanaeshwar and others. In this way, the entire Hindu society through the length and breadth of the country was knit together by the thread of Bhakti, which enabled it to withstand the surge of Islamism during the long period of Muslim rule: More of it in the next chapter.

13

Bhakti Poets as Saviours of Hinduism

The leading lights of Bhakti ideology and literature during the Middle Ages were Kabir Das, Raidas, Soordas and Tulsi Das. It is these saint poets who proved to be the saviours of the great Hindu civilization during the darkest period of its chequered history. The rich treasure of popular Bhakti or devotional literature created by them touching the hearts of the common people fortified the Hindu masses against the relentless surge of Islamism during the period.

Kabir Das (1398-1518) was born at Kashi (Varanasi) in a 'Julaha' or weaver family of Muslim background. The "Julahas" were originally Hindus belonging to the weaver caste known as "Kori" who had converted to Islam. The culture and traditions of his family were thus substantially Hindu, which largely influenced his thoughts and observations. Accordingly, he took to Bhakti-Yoga himself and spread the message of love of Rama, the God Supreme, among the masses through his poetic observations.

But his Rama or God Supreme was "Nirakar" or formless, not embodied in any idol or image. His Rama is "Param Brahman" or the Supreme Soul of Vedanta of whom every individual soul is a fragment. The only way to merge into the "Param Brahman" and attain salvation is Bhakti or pure love of God. He became an apostle and mouthpiece of the socially downtrodden people by forcefully advocating complete equality of all in pursuit of their devotion to the God Supreme. He came down heavily against the evils like untouchability and social inequality corroding the Hindu society which the Islamists were taking advantage of. His pithy couplets composed in simple, almost rustic, Hindi contained profound wisdom and had tremendous appeal among the common people. He thus prevented large number of the socially disadvantaged sections from being lured into Islam.

Sant Raidas (1376-1527) was born at Kashi (Varanasi) in a family of "Chamar" (Shoe-maker) caste. Early in his life, he became a devotee of Rama and Krishna and was accepted by Swami Ramananda as his close disciple. But like in case of Kabir Das, his Rama and Krishna were not identical with or confined to their idols in temples. His Rama was the "Nirakar" or formless God Supreme residing in every individual soul. He dedicated his entire life to Bhakti or devotion to his universal Rama. In one of his odes to God, he observed that his God needed him as much as he needed him.

Thanks to the reforming zeal of Swami Ramanand and the liberal trend set by him, the "Chamar" caste background was no handicap to Sant Raidas. Impressed by his Bhakti or devotion to God, the Raja of Kashi became his disciple. The Jhali Rani, wife of Maharana Udai Singh of Chittour, also became his disciple. The famous Krishna bhakta Meerabai, the Mewar Princess, also accepted Sant Raidas as her spiritual guru. That incidentally symbolized the integral unity of the concepts of "Nirgun" or formless god (Kabir and Raidas) and "Sagun" Krishna and Rama of Meera, Tulsidas and others.

The wide acceptance of Raidas as a great saint irrespective of his caste background brought respectability to the so-called lower castes. Thereby his Bhakti helped in consolidating the unity of Hindu society which worked as a bulwark against the tide of Islamism. Sant Raidas, in fact, directly rebuffed the Islamists who tried to coax and cajole him into accepting Islam. Sikandar Lodi is reported to have even sent threats to him to convert to Islam or face punishment, but he stubbornly refused to be cowed down. It was in response to such overt pressures that he wrote "when Vedic religion is the best and pure source of knowledge, why should I give up the true faith and read Quran ?". That was a rebuff to Islamism loud and clear.

Bhakta Soor Das (1478-1580) was born blind in a village near the sacred town of Mathura. His congenital handicap of blindness, however, did not deter him from turning out to be the most illustrious representative of Bhakti poets. Having been born near Mathura, it was but natural for him to become an ardent devotee of Lord Krishna. His most notable poetic work dedicated to Lord Krishna is 'Soor Sagar'. Said to have originally contained around a hundred thousand verses, only about six thousand verses have come down to us as gems of Bhakti poetry.

Like Kabir and Raidas, he also held that every individual soul is a fragment of "Param Brahman" or the Supreme God. And like them, he emphatically rejected the caste hierarchy professing complete equality of all in the eyes of god. But while Kabir and Raidas were worshippers of "Nirgun" or formless God, Soordas was a devotee of "Sagun" God in the form of Krishna. He adopted "Braj-bhasa", the spoken Hindi of the Mathura region, as the medium of his devotional poetry which made it very popular. His poems were widely recited by a host of "bhajan" singers which touched the hearts of the people throughout North India. So much so that some open-hearted Muslims, free from the fanaticism of Islamism, like Raskhan also became devotees of Lord Krishna.

Soor Das had drawn inspiration from his contemporary Sri Ballabhacharya who was engaged in spreading Krishna-bhakti or devotion to Lord Krishna across the country. This was a time when the Islamists were destroying temples and idols of Hindu gods ruthlessly. It was in such a difficult situation that Sri Ballabhacharya carried the original idol of Shri Nathjee (Lord Krishna) from Mathura region to the safe zone of Aravali hills in Mewar. It was here that he got the idol installed and the famous Sri Nath temple constructed at Nathdwara about 25 kms from Udaipur. The temple, which is an important place of pilgrimage for Hindus from all over the world, is a standing monument of Islamic assault and Hindu resistance.

It was given to Goswami Tulsi Das (1497-1623) to make Ram-bhakti or devotion to Lord Rama, a household affair for Hindus across the country. Like other great Hindu saints referred to earlier, Tulsi Das lived and studied scriptures away from home from an early age. For around 15 years, he lived in the Ashram of Swamy Ramananda at Panch Ganga Ghat in Kashi (Varanasi) studying the Vedas, Upanishads, history etc. He married Ratna Devi and was in deep love with her, but gave up family life after sometime and dedicated himself totally to bhakti of Lord Rama. He visited all the four "Dhams" or holy places of Hindu pilgrimage in the four corners of the country and returned back to Varanasi to produce his most precious gift to Hindu society - the Ramayan.

Although he was an erudite Sanskrit scholar, he took to spoken Hindi (Awadhi) to render the story of Lord Rama in his epic work for easy access to the heart of Hindu masses. And it worked. The "Dohas" (couplets) and "Choupais" (Quarduplets) of his Ramayana became household words in every Hindu home in large parts of the country. They contained not only the life story of Lord Rama as an incarnation of God but also words of wisdon for every human being to emulate. The worldly life and conduct of Rama, Sita, Lakshman and Bharat became an ideal which is still cherished by the Indian people in general.

The bhakti of "Nirgun" Rama (formless God) preached by Kabir and Raidas had limited appeal to minds which could conceptualise a formless God. On the other hand, it was much easier for the common people to visualize a "Sagun" Rama in human form and worship him as their divine benefactor and protector against all odds. Of all the bhakti poets, it was Tulsidas who made bhakti or devotion to Rama as an "Avtar" of god most wide-spread and popular among the masses as well as the classes.

Taken together, the Bhakti poets of the Middle Ages provided the most protective shield of religion of the heart to Hindu masses against the unceasing onslaught of Islamism. If temples were being demolished and idols broken, they could install idols of their deities in their own homes and worship them. The practice has continued right up to this day whereby every ordinary Hindu household has a corner reserved for worship of their cherished deities. This is a legacy of those dark days when the very existence of temples was threatened. If they were unable to worship in a temple at a public place, they would have a temple in every home. It was the bhakti movement which enabled them to resort to this practice which is unique among all the notable religions of the world. A Christian has to go to a church and a Muslim to a mosque, but a Hindu can worship god in his own home.

14

The Sikh Gurus

Any account of Bhakti Movement as an impregnable shield against the attack of Islamism would be incomplete without the heroic tale of Sikh Gurus. While the saint poets referred to earlier provided the Hindu masses with an immune system against the challenge of Islamism indirectly through the message of bhakti, the Sikh gurus confronted it headlong directly in a more telling way. And they had to pay a heavy price for their bold defiance of the dictates of Islamists in blood and tears. The bhakti poets were wielding their pen in quiet seclusion; the Sikh gurus had to face the sword of Islamists in the open and make the ultimate sacrifice of life in defence of the faith.

Sri Nanak Deo Jee (1469-1539), the First Guru, started with the tradition of bhakti sweeping the Hindu society at that time and carried it forward to unprecedented heights. He stands out not only as the tallest and most influential among bhakti poets, but also as the founder of a reformed faith cleansed of the flab of caste-based inequality which was corroding the Hindu Society. In one of his poetic observations, he says: "I keep company with the lowest among the most lowly castes... your (god's) grace lies where the lowly castes are well looked after". Like Kabir and Raidas, he believed in the "Nirakar" (formless) God Supreme corresponding to the "Brahman" or the Supreme Soul of Vedanta.

As a true seeker after the Ultimate Reality or "Param Brahman", Sri Nanak Deo jee went on pilgrimage to all the Hindu holy places like Mathura, Brindaban, Ayodhya, Gaya and Rameswaram. He also visited the Muslim holy places like Mecca and Madina with a band of dedicated disciples. They came from all castes and lived and dined together without any discrimination. In the process, the caste identities of the pilgrims and all social divisions between high and low were completely obliterated. That was a revolutionary development at the time.

What distinguishes Guru Nanak Deojee from other bhakti poets is his strong reaction to the savage assault of Islamism on the Hindu society. In his own life time, he was a witness to the brutality of Sikander Lodi against the Hindus and their places of worship. He had also seen the ravages of Baber and destruction of Saidpur during his attack on the Punjab. He was so stung by it that he remonstrates with the Creator (God) how He remained a mute spectator to the atrocities and destructions caused by Mughal Babar. His anguish and plea with God in this regard find expression in the holy "Guru Granth Sahib" (Asa Mahala, page 360). The result was that he laid the foundation of a vibrant religious order - the Sikh Panth - to take on the might of Islamism.

It was the fifth Guru, Sri Arjun Deoji, who collected the hymnal prayers of Sri Guru Nanak and scriptures of the other gurus before him and compiled the sacred book - Sri Guru Granth Sahib. The book was written in the Punjabi script that is known as Gurumukhi (Script of the Gurus). Besides the golden words of the Sikh Gurus, the holy book incorporates the spiritual observations of devotional poets like Kabir Das, Raidas, Namdeo,

Ramanand, Soor Das and others in best tradition of bhakti literature. Accordingly, the name of Lord Rama occurs more than 2000 times, of "Par Brhman" over 500 times, of "Onkar" about 400 times and of Veda, Purana and other Hindu scriptures 500 times in Guru Granth Sahib. Apart from compilation of the holy book, Guru Arjun Deoji is highly revered for his supreme sacrifice in defence of the faith against the attack of Islamism. Unnerved by his growing popularity, the Mughal Emperor Jehangir called him to Lahore and ordered him to embrace Islam. On his firm refusal to do so, he was put to inhuman torture like being made to sit on a hot iron pot and burning with heated sand. He suffered all the brutalities bravely praying to God, but stubbornly refused to accept Islam and made the ultimate sacrifice of his life.

But that was not the end of Mughal rulers' barbarities against the Sikh gurus and their followers in pursuit of Islamism. The worst was to follow during the regime of Aurangzeb. The 9th Guru, Shri Teg Bahadurji, was arrested at Sirhind in Punjab alongwith his three trusted associates - Bhai Mati Das, Bhai Sati Das and Bhai Dayala. They were brought to Delhi and confined in the Kotwali where the diabolical process of torture began. The royal Qazi directed the Kotwal to leave no stone unturned to convert them to Islam. Accordingly, Sri Guru Teg Bahadur was kept thirsty for three days without a drop of water, pressed against a heated pillar and sprayed with red hot sand. But like Guru Arjun Deoji, earlier, he refused to accept Islam.

Similar fate awaited his three loyal followers. The royal Qazi asked them to either convert to Islam or face death. All the three refused to be converted. Then, under royal orders, they were put to death one by one in the most cruel manner. Bhai Mati Das was cut into pieces by saw, Bhai Sati Das was thrown into a tub of boiling water and Bhai Dayala was wrapped with cotton and burnt to death. On 11 November 1675,

Aurangzeb himself ordered Guru Teg Bahadur to embrace Islam. On his firm refusal, the guru was made to sit under a tree in the Kotwali premises and beheaded by sword.

In Delhi's Chandni Chowk, there is a place now called "Bhai Mati Das Chowk" opposite the celebrated Gurudwara Shishganj. During Mughal times, Delhi Kotwali (Police Station) was located there. Few people recall today that this is the place where the tragic drama of barbarous cruelty was enacted at the behest of the Mughal Emperor in pursuit of Islamism over 330 years ago. The brutal torture and beheading of Guru Teg Bahadur by the Mughals was no less heinous than the crucification of Christ by the Romans over 2006 years ago.

The martyrdom of Guru Teg Bahadur ignited a flame that wreaked havoc on Aurangzeb's Mughal forces. His son Guru Govind Singhji, the 10th and last guru, vowed to pay back the Islamists in their own coins by matching sword with sword in defence of the Hindu civilization. He transformed his devout followers into an "Army of the Pure" (Khalsa) and himself took the surname "Singh" (Lion) to take on the Mughal lmperial Islamists. He also baptized his foremost disciples with the same designation of "Singh" which members of the Sikh community adopt even today. To wield his "Khalsa" into a band of human lions to fight the Mughal tyranny, he prescribed five symbols to signify the martial form of Sikhism: uncut hair, a "Kanghi" (Comb) to control it, a sword or dagger (Kripan), a steel bracelet (Kada) to be worn on one's right wrist and shorts (Kachha) to enable Sikh-lions to jump on horseback and gallop into battle. These five signs (Kachha, Kirpan, Kada, Kesh and Comb) which are still the distinguishing marks of a Sikh, epitomize the gurus' heroic fight against Aurangazeb's imperial Islamism.

Apart from his martial response to Islamic tyranny in defence of the Hindu civilization, guru Govind Singhji also contributed significantly to the consolidation of Hindu society by wielding together all castes, high and low, into his Khalsa (Army of the pure). His first five soldiers of the "Khalsa" were Dayaram Khatri of Lahore, second Dharam Das Jat of Delhi, third Mahakam Chand Washerman of Dwarika, fourth Himmat, Cook of Jagannathpuri and fifth Saheb Chand barber of Beedar. That was a symbolic step signifying the complete rejection of caste hierarchy which had long been a bane of Hindu Society. Sikhism thus, as shaped by Guru Gobind Singhji, emerged as the strongest armour to counter the most virulent attack of Islamism under the imperial regime of Aurangzeb.No wonder that Swamy Vivekanand was to tell his followers later "Remember, if you wish to do good to your country, then each one of you will have to become Sri Guru Gobind Singh".

The Guruji had to pay a heavy price for his bold and courageous counter - offensive against imperial Islamism. His sons were either killed in battle or executed in prison by Aurangzeb's forces. He himself was assassinated by two Muslims in October, 1708, a year after Aurangzeb's death. But before that, he had declared an end to the line of living Gurus and established Sri Guru Granth Sahib, the holy book, as the Supreme spiritual symbol or Deity of Sikhs.

15

The New Era of Hindu Rennaissance

The inherent spiritual strength of Hinduism enabled it to survive protracted depredations of Islamism for well over 600 years. It emerged badly bruised and shaken but not vanished at the end of the long dark age of Islamic rule. The Islamic era finally came to an end not long after the death in 1707 of Aurangzeb, the most fanatic Islamist of all the Mughal rulers of India. That brought about the new dawn of a fresh Hindu awakening which may be termed as Hindu Renaissance. It threw up a series of enlightened Hindu religious-cum-social reformers who breathed a new life into the age-old Hindu civilization.

In about 50 years after Aurangzeb's passing away, the Islamists' disintegrated in the face of strong resistance by Sikhs, Rajputs and Marathas under the umbrella of the time-honored Hindu civilization. They were ousted from power but the vacuum so created came to be filled up by the British colonialists. As Jawahar Lal Nehru has summed up, "The Mughal Empire was not overthrown by the British, but by these religious nationalist movements" *('Glimpses of World History'* by J.L. Nehru).

The establishment of British colonial rule in India was a part of the process of empire-building in which the European countries were engaged at that time. It was primarily a matter of their commercial expansion and economic exploitation of the colonial countries by the imperial powers. Although it was a secular exercise with no overt religious overtone, yet it did contribute to the spread of Christianity - the religion of the Imperial Countries — in an indirect sort of way. For wherever the conquering Imperial Powers went, Christian Missionaries followed them with their own objective of converting the local people to Christianity. While the Colonial rulers indulged in empire building and economic exploitation of the people they ruled over, Christian missionaries pursued their own agenda of spreading Christianity. This was a common practice in all parts of the world which came under the grip of European imperialists. India was no exception.

Accordingly, with the advent of British rule, Christian Missionaries started large-scale operation of converting Indian people to their faith which posed a fresh threat to Hinduism. For Christianity is as proselytizing a religion as Islam, if not more. A significant difference however is that while the Islamists resorted to the sword and the might of political power, as in the case of India and elsewhere, the Christian Missionaries sought to do it by quiet but dogged persuasion, preaching and temptation combined with doses of social service.

The most visible effect of Christian Missionaries' operation was found in Bengal, which was the seat of British imperial power during the 19th century. Impressed by the scientific knowledge and social advancement of the British as well as the glitter of the Raj, a good number of Bengali elite turned towards Christianity. They were the English educated people who were repelled by such social evils as Sati, enforced widowhood, untouchability and polygamy in the orthodox Hindu society.

But whenever the abiding Hindu Civilization was faced with any such threat or challenge, as in the past, it threw up a socio-religious reformer or movement to ward off the challenge.

This time round in Bengal, it was Raja Ram Mohan Roy (1774-1833) who took note of the challenge of Christian Missionaries and thwarted their mission in his own way. Coming from an elite Brahmin family of Bengal, and equipped with the best traditions of 19th century western liberalism, he turned out to be a great social and religious reformer. He worked tirelessly, inspite of hostility from orthodox circles, to rid the Hindu society of evils like Sati, untouchability etc and came out boldly in support of widow re-marriage. As a man of religion, he studied the Upanishads and translated some of them into Bengali. He believed in universalist Hinduism based on the Upanishadic worship of a formless God.

As a counter to the Christian Missionaries, Raja Ram Mohan Roy sought to institutionalize his concept of Upanishadic Hinduism to widen its base among the English educated Bengalis leaning towards Christianity. To this end, he founded a religious order known as Brahmo Samoj in 1828. It was dedicated to the "Worship and adoration of Eternal, Un-searchable and Immaculate Being, who is the Author and Preserver of the Universe". He threw open the Samaj to all irrespective of caste, creed, colour and nationality, thereby seeking to establish a universal faith on the Hindu base.

After the death of Raja Ram Moham Roy, in 1833, Debendra Nath Tagore (1817-1905), father of Rabindra Nath Tagore, further organized the Brahmo Samaj by elaborating the Upanishadic concept of one "Supreme Being, the God of Truth, Infinite Wisdom" whose worship leads to salvation. The principal contribution of Brahmo Samaj was that it prevented the modernist English educated Bengali people from drifting towards

Christianity by providing them with a reformed spiritual platform under the broad canopy of Hinduism.

While Brahmo Samaj was effectively shielding the Bengali intellectual class from drifting towards Christianity, another great saviour of Hinduism emerged from Gujarat in Western India. This was Swamy Dayanand Saraswati (1824-1883). Coming from a well-to-do orthodox Brahmin family, he renounced family life early and came over to Mathura to study the Hindu scriptures. After three years of deep studies under his blind guru Swamy Virijanandji, he came out to preach the pure Vedic religion without the admixture of Puranas, Shastras, tantra etc. His cry was "Back to the Veda", pure and unadulterated.

Towards this end, Swamy Dayanand founded the religious order known as "Arya Samaj" in 1875 at Bombay and later shifted its headquarters to Lahore in Punjab. It was here that he wrote his great gospel "Satyarth Prakash" (The Torch Light of Truth) in which the Bible was put to severe criticism. He vehemently criticized the caste hierarchy and his Arya Samaj emerged as a great champion of the untouchables and their right to enter any and all holy temples.

Like Raja Ram Mohan Roy, Swami Dayanandji was not only a religious but also a great social reformer. As such, he rooted for complete equality between men and women and people from all castes in receiving education, study of the Vedas and performing religious rites. He initiated large numbers of untouchables and women as "Purohits" (priests) who not only studied the Vedas but also performed Vedic rites like "Yagayas", For him, religious and social reforms were part of the same process of rejuvenation of the Hindu society.

His reforming zeal also had a strong nationalist component. He was very much against any foreign cultural invasion. As a nationalist Hindu, he was strongly opposed to the spread of Christianity and Islam. As such, he initiated the "Shuddhi" (reconversion) movement, whereby people who had been converted to Islam or Christianity could be brought back to Hinduism.

The agenda of Arya Samaj set by Swamy Dayanandji was carried forward with full vigour by his disciple Swamy Shraddhanandji (1856-1926). Born at Jallundhar, Punjab, and a qualified lawyer, he gave up his practice of law and committed himself wholly to promoting the religious and social reforms ideology of Arya Samaj. Apart from propagating the pure Vedic religion, Swamy Shraddhanand plunged into the task of upliftment of "Dalits" (untouchables) and women in a big way. Thousands of Dalits were initiated into performing Vedic rituals and adorned with the sacred thread, claimed to be the privilege of Brahmins only. For advancement of women's education, he founded the Kanya Pathshala (girls school) at Jallundhar in 1888 which later grew into a full-fledged women's university (Kanya Maha Vidyalaya). The famous Gurukul was established at Kangri (Haridwar) in 1902 which was open to Dalits and other down trodden castes.

Above all, he carried the Shuddhi movement, initiated by Swamy Dayanand, to its logical conclusion. In Gudiwara, about 3000 Dalits who had been converted to Christianity were initiated back to Hinduism according to Vedic rites. The biggest event happened at Agra where about two lakh people who had converted to Islam were brought back to the Hindu fold in a mass ceremony. The Shuddhi movement got great momentum in North India under the patronage of Arya Samaj led by Swami Shraddhanandji. Being annoyed at this development, an Islamist— Abdul Rashid - assassinated him on 23rd December, 1926.

Thus, Arya Samaj, during the time of Swami Dayanand and Swami Shraddhananda, became some sort of a mass movement. This was in sharp contrast to Brahmo Samaj, the other reform movement which had emerged in Bengal at that time, which remained confined to Bengali intellectuals only. The nationalist component of Arya Samaj made it a part of the upsurge of nationalism which was stirring India in late 19th and early 20th centuries. Many ardent followers of Arya Samaj were also part of the national movement for freedom. Their religion of the Veda was deemed as a nationalist religion.

The socio-religious reform movements of late 19th and early 20th centuries actually prepared the ground for India's freedom movement to take off subsequently in full steam. In fact, the early stalwarts of our struggle for independence like Bal Gangadhar Tilak, Lala Lajpat Rai, Madan Mohan Malviya and others were all thrown up by the socio-religious reform movements that preceded it.

16

Swami Rama Krishna Paramhans : The Spiritual Fountain Spring of Hindu Revival

While Arya Samaj was making strides in the Country's heartland, another great spiritual genius was making waves in Bengal. He was Swami Rama Krishna Paramhans (1836-1886). Born as Gadadhar Thakur in Kamarpukur near Kolkata, Rama Krishna took to asceticism at a very early age. He used to fall into "Samadhi" since his childhood which became more intense as he matured into a full-fledged "Sanyasi". He attained complete unity with "Brahman" or "Supreme Soul" of Vedanta in the state of "Nirvikalpaka Samadhi" during which he remained motionless with almost stoppage of heart-beat.

As a result of his supreme spiritual realization, Swami Rama Krishna propounded that "Brahman" or Supreme Godhead is manifest in many forms of religious deities worshipped by Hindus. "Brahman" is also un-manifest or formless as envisaged in Vedanta of Hindus or held by Christians and Muslims. In fact, he practiced and experienced in his vision all religions - Islam, Christianity, and Hinduism in all its diverse manifestations - and found that "it is the same God towards whom all are directing their steps, though along different paths." That was an eloquent exposition of the inclusive and universalist character of Hindu Civilization by one of its most spiritually enlightened sage gurus.

Even though he found his highest spiritual experience in "Samadhi", he made clear that it is not the end-all and be-all of life. "Samadhi" must initiate people into service of mankind to alleviate human suffering. He is reported to have said: "Are you seeking God? Then seek Him in Man. The divinity is manifest in man more than in any other object". He believed in the unity of all religions and service to the whole of mankind.

That infact has been the core value of the universalist Hindu civilization which has enabled it to withstand persistent attacks from other organized single track religions in its long history. The very diversity of its ways to realize God and modes of worship is the greatest strength and beauty of Hinduism. Swami Ram Krishna's broad view about the unity of religions was elaborated later by Sri Aurobindo in 1909. Talking about enlightened Hinduism, he observed that "it is in the first place a non-dogmatic inclusive religion and would have taken even Islam and Christianity into itself, if they had tolerated the process".

Of the twin principles of unity of all religions and service of mankind, Swami Ram Krishna practiced and realized the first himself. As for the second, he raised an army of "Sanyasis" to carry out his mission. The Chief among them was Swami Vivekananda who was entrusted with the task of educating the world in spiritual enlightenment and service to fellow human beings to alleviate human suffering. Towards the end of his life,

Swami Ram Krishna gave the following instruction to Swami Vivekananda: "You will bring spiritual consciousness to men and assuage the misery of the humble and poor." More about Swamy Vivekananda in the next chapter.

The common practice of idol worship by Hindu masses, which had been under severe physical attack by Islamists during Muslim rule, came under fresh intellectual challenge from Westerners during the 19th century. The Adi Brahmo Samaj founded by Raja Ram Mohan Roy sought to meet the challenge by giving up idol worship even while retaining the primacy of Hinduism. He dedicated his Samaj to the worship of the Eternal Being "Who is the Author and Preserver of the Universe". But Swami Ram Krishna was to observe later that the attributes of being the Author and Preserver of the Universe are merely hard and petrified forms of God, which do not render him formless. He pithily remarked that the Brahmo concept of God was really a subtle form of idol worship. He himself worshipped Mother Kali and found her as much formless as in the form of a deity.

A large number of intellectuals including many prominent Brahmo Samajis came to him or were in regular communication with him. The most notable among them was Keshab Chandra Sen (1834-1884) who took over the mantle of Brahmo Samaj and changed the whole tenor and texture of Adi Brahmo Samaj. He started as a great admirer of Christ and sought to "Christianize Hinduism" and 'Hinduize Christianity'. But coming under the influence of Swami Ram Krishna, he not only stuck to his Hindu spiritual heritage but much more. He ended up as a worshipper of God as Mother and introduced "Kirtan" (devotional song) into his mode of worship. Thus he revived the Bhakti tradition of Chaitanya Maha Prabhu which had shielded Hinduism in Bengal in earlier centuries from growing power of Islam.

It was under the strong influence of Swami Rama Krishna that Keshab Chandra Sen finalized his religious position in his New Dispensation (Nava Vidhan) in January 1880. Worship of God as Mother and assimilation of much of Hindu polytheism (worship of more than one God) into Brahmoism were the key components of Keshab Chandra Sen's New Dispensation. These were clearly the outcome of Swami Ram Krishna's impact on him. For according to the Swami, worship of any symbol of God is just as valid as worship of the formless God.

Implicit in his worship of Mother Kali's idol was the question whether he was worshipping a piece of stone or a living Goddess. And he was assured through intense spiritual experience several times that She was real, She was present, the Mother Goddess he was worshipping. As for the worship of God in different names like Shiva, Vishnu and Shakti by Hindus, he observed that "Brahman" (the God Supreme) is Shiva and Shakti both in one. He exemplified it in his own life and personality. He adopted the name Ram Krishna which is clearly Vaishnavite, both Rama and Krishna being incarnations of Vishnu. And yet he was a devotee of Goddess Shakti in the form of Mother Kali. That incidentally underlined the essential unity of diverse sects of Hinduism.

Romain Rolland, the great French Savant and intellectual, observed that "the Paramhansa - the Indian Swan - rested his great white wings on the sapphire lake of eternity beyond the veil of tumultuous days". In his book "The Life of Ramakrishna", he summed up. "The man whose image I here evoke was the consummation of two thousand years of the spiritual life of three hundred million people (than the population of India). He was no hero of action like Gandhi, no genius in art or thought like Goethe or Tagore. He was a little Brahmin of Bengal, whose outer life was set in a limited frame without striking incident, outside the political and social activities of his time. But his inner life embraced the whole multiplicity of men and Gods".

And yet Swami Rama Krishna's influence was crucial in this period for a Hindu revival in Bengal. This was a time when Hinduism faced a huge intellectual challenge from westerners and their Indian admirers. His universalist religious philosophy restored the faith of the intellectual class in the basics of Hinduism.

Above all, his impact on growing Indian nationalism, though indirect, cannot be ignored. He symbolized a strong national identity in the face of a foreign Colonial power that was intellectually undermining the very foundations of Indianness. The concept of Mother India, which stirred the hearts of freedom fighters in those days like nothing else, was an extension of the worship of Mother Goddess by Swami Rama Krishna. Infact, Bankim Chandra Chatterjee's celebrated song "Vande Mataram", which narrowly missed being made the official national anthem after independence, was an out-growth of Swami Rama Krishna's Mother Goddess symbolism.

The remarkable contribution of Swami Ram Krishna and his most illustrious disciple Vivekanand to India's national regeneration has been well brought out by another western writer - Amoury de Riencourt. He writes: "The greatest leaders of the early twentieth century, whatever their walk of lives - Rabindranath Tagore, the prince of poets, Aurobindo Ghosh, the greatest mystic philosopher, Mahatma Gandhi, who eventually shook the Anglo-Indian Empire to destruction - all acknowledged their overriding debt to both the Swan and the Eagle, to Rama Krishna who stirred the heart of India, and to Vivekananda who awakened its soul".

17

Swami Vivekanand, The Torch Bearer of Rennaissant Hinduism

It was given to Swami Vivekanand (1863-1902) to build the magnificent edifice of rennaissant Hinduism on the deep spiritual foundation laid by Swami Ram Krishna Paramhans. He carried forward the great spiritual heritage of his guru to such heights that not only protected the ancient Hindu civilization from western intellectual challenges in India but dazzled the West itself. He brought about a beautiful synthesis of the doctrines of Advaita (non-dualism) highlighted by Adi Shankaracharya and Dvaita (Dualism) of Madhavacharya, Gyan Marg (path of knowledge) and Bhakti Marg (the path of devotional worship) and even idol worship as stages in attaining "Moksha" or oneness with "Brahman" (God).

He observed: "As absolute, Brahman alone is true; as relative truth, all the different sects, standing upon different manifestations of the same Brahman, either in India or elsewhere, are true. Only some are higher than others............

And as the Vedas are only scriptures which teach this real absolute God, of which all other ideas of God are but minimized and limited visions and as all other religions represent one or other of these stages in an unprogressive and crystallized form, all the other religions of the world are included in the nameless, limitless, eternal Vedic religion". ("In defense of Hinduism" by Swami Vivekanand, published by Advaita Ashram, 12th impression-1999).

Born of Bengali Kayastha parents at Kolkata in 1863, Narendra Nath Dutta (his original name) was a boy of precocious mind and keen intellect. Being good at studies and sports, he was a leader among his group of friends in school. In 1880, he joined the Scottish Church College, Calcutta, where he studied Western Philosophy and history of European nations. It was during this period that questions about the existence of God started stirring his mind. This led him first to congregational prayers of Keshab Chandra Sen's Brahmo Samaj and finally to Swami Ramakrishna of Dakshineshwar. After considerable questioning and arguments, Narendra finally accepted Swami Rama Krishna as his spiritual guru whole-heartedly. It was Swami Rama Krishna who synthesized all manifestations of Hinduism like Dvaita (Dualism), Advaita (Non-dualism), Bhakti and idol worship into one spiritual whole. While he primarily taught dualism and Bhakti to his other disciples, he satisfied Narendra's rationalist mind by initiating him into the depths of Advaita Vedanta or the philosophy of Non-dualism.

Narendra had a forceful personality, with his imposing body and sharp intellect, which concealed a constant inner struggle. He wanted to dominate everything and renounce everything, that is, to have both the world and God. When his strong personality evoked mistrust among others, Swami Rama Krishna, who knew better, remarked: "The day when Naren comes in contact with suffering and misery, the pride of his character will melt into a mood of infinite compassion. His strong faith in himself will be an instrument to re-establish in discouraged souls the confidence and faith they have lost".

This observation of the Master was prophetic, as all the powers, ambitions and desires of Narendra renamed Vivekanand were harnessed into the mission of service to suffering humanity. His supermost goal came to be : "a religion which will give us faith in ourselves, a national self-respect, and the power to feed and educate the poor and relieve the misery around me
If you want to find God, serve man" (quoted in "The Life of Vivekanand" by Romain Rolland, 21st Impression-2004). About five years of spiritual education and experience under Swami Rama Krishna from November 1881 to August 1886 transformed Narendra completely. From a dominating, restless and impatient youth, he turned into a mature Sanyasi who was ready to renounce everything for God-realization and service to suffering humanity. After his Master's death in August 1886, Narendra and a core group of Swami Rama Krishna's disciples vowed to become monks and renounce all material sinews of living. They started living the life of wandering monks, like Sidharth Gautam (the Buddha) centuries earlier, with no other possession than their robes and begging bowls.

In July 1890, Narendra broke loose from his spiritual home at Baranagore, where he had set himself up after the departure of his Master, and set upon a journey which was to take him through to the length and breadth of the country. He sought the blessings of the "Holy Mother" (Widow of Swami Rama Krishna) and wanted to take retreat in the Himalayas for solitary contemplation. But the tragic death of a sister reminded him of the sacrificial fate of a Hindu woman and the innumerable problems of his people. He was thrown back from the cool and silence of Himalayas to the heat and noise of human living. He fell seriously ill twice at Rudraprayag and Hrishikesh and narrowly escaped death, reminiscent of the fate of Adi Shankaracharya during his journey centuries earlier. But he continued his journey, leaving Delhi alone in February 1891.

His continuous journey took him to Rajasthan, Gujarat, Maharasthra, Kerala, Karnataka and Tamil Nadu. In course of his journey, he stayed in King's palaces and huts of the poor. He came in close contact with the culture of different regions of India and their Gods and Goddesses as manifestations of only one God. To the intellectuals obsessed with the abstract, he preached respect for images and idols of Gods, and to the people in general, a sacred love for mother India. He reached Kanyakumari, the southernmost tip of India, on 24 December 1892. There he swam across the sea and meditated on a lone rock away from the mainland.

After three days of meditation, he swam back to the coast of India and came over by foot to Madras. And there in early 1893, he declared his wish to carry forward his mission to the Western world. The idea was widely welcomed by all - the rich and the poor, the Raja of Ramanad and Maharaja of Khetri, and the swelling number of his disciples. They helped him to set out on his journey to the U.S.A. to represent Hinduism in the world parliament of Religions at Chicago. It was the Maharaja of Khetri who gave him the name of Vivekanand when he was about to proceed to America and the name stuck to him.

The first session of the World Parliament of Religions attended by thousands of delegates opened at Chicago on 11 September 1893 with due solemnity. When Swami Vivekanand took his turn to speak towards the end of the day, a flame went through the audience. Bowing to Sarasvati, the Goddess of wisdom, he addressed them as "Sisters and Brothers of America". It touched the hearts of the assembled thousands who rose in their seats and gave him loud applause which lasted for about two minutes.

He began by thanking the youngest of nations (the U.S.) on behalf of the oldest monastic order of the world, the Vedic order of Sanyasis. He told the audience how India had always given shelter to religious refugees of other lands like the Israelites and Zoroastrians, which highlighted its ethos of universal toleration. He presented Hinduism as the mother of religions which taught the twin principles : "Accept and understand one another". And he quoted two passages from Hindu scriptures: "Whoever comes to me, through whatsoever form, I reach him". "All men are struggling through paths which in the end lead to Me".

There could be no better exposition of the universalist character of Hinduism. Each of the other speaker was speaking of the God of his sect. Vivekanand alone spoke of all their Gods and embraced them all in the one Universal Being. The American Press recognized him as "the greatest figure in the Parliament of Religions. After hearing him we feel how foolish it is to send missionaries to this learned nation". (Quoted in "The Life of Vivekananda" by Romain Rolland: 21st Impression - 2004). Thus his learned discourse at the Parliament of Religions, which he addressed about a dozen times, raised India identified by its universalist Hindu Civilization, to a high pedestal in the eyes of the world.

No wonder that he was widely hailed in America and the western world and spent around four years lecturing and touring. He not only kindled western interest in Hinduism but also introduced Yoga and Vedanta in the West and started Vedantic centers in New York City and London.

After constant lecturing and winning disciples in the western world, Swami Vivekanand returned back to India in early 1897. And in May 1897, he founded one of the most extensive spiritual and humanitarian monastic orders in India named Rama Krishna Mission. It's key objective was to work "for the establishment of fellowship among the followers of different religions, knowing them all to be only so many forms of one undying eternal religion", the Sanatan Dharma.

He toured the west once again during 1899 and 1900 spreading the message of spirituality and humanitarianism. He highlighted the Rama Krishna Mission's emphasis on service to others as "Karma Yoga", which is a basic concept of Hinduism. He thus not only adequately met the western challenge to Hinduism but also initiated many westerners into the basics of the Hindu faith.

On his second home-coming from the West, he plunged into his hectic work schedule without taking a break. He went up to Mayawati in the hills to visit the Advaita Ashram where his western disciple-Captain Sevier had died. He came back to Belur Math after consoling his disciple's widow and talking to the inmates of the Ashram. But there was no rest for him. In response to pressing calls, he travelled to Dacca, Guwahati and Shillong. His constant tours and crushing work-schedule took a toll on his failing health.

On 4 July 1902, he meditated in his room at Belur Math in the forenoon, dined with the inmates at midday, taught Sanskrit grammar to his pupils in the afternoon, went on a long walk with a brother-monk in the evening and meditated for an hour in his room early in the night. And shortly after 9 p.m., he passed away, his soul leaving his body, at the young age of 39 years. Thus like a true Karma Yogi that he was, Swami Vivekananda was as tightly engaged in his work, if not more, on his last day on this earth as he had been through the rest of his life. And like Adi Shankaracharya who did so much to rejuvenate Hinduism in a short life span of 32 years during ancient times, Swami Vivekananda turned out to be the greatest apostle of modern Hindu awakening in his short life span of 39 years.

18

Vivekanand's Concept of Indian Nationalism

Swamy Vivekanda was hailed in India and the world for his over-powering spiritualism and innate humanism. Beginning with his momentous address at the Parliament of Religions in America, he came to be widely acknowledged as a great spiritual Guru in the Western world. He won a large number of admirers and disciples in America and Europe who were overwhelmed by Adi Shankaracharya's Vedanta as elaborated by him. Prominent among them were the famous German Indologist Max Muller and Paul Deussen, Professor of Philosophy at the University of Kiel, Germany. Professor Paul Deussen held that the system of Vedanta founded on the Upanishads was one of the "most majestic structures and valuable products of the genius of man in his search for truth..."

Among his well known western disciples were Miss Margaret Noble, (Sister Nivedita), Mr. Sturdy, Captain Sevier and his wife. The latter couple actually came over to India and lived at Advaita Ashram set up by the Swami at Mayawati in

Himalayan foothills for the rest of their lives. Margaret Noble had this to say about the impact of Vivekananda's teachings in England : "To not a few of us, the words of Swami Vivekananda came as living water to men perishing of thirst... .The people that walked in darkness have seen a great light... .." (Quoted in "Vivekananda: A Biography" by Swami Nikhilananda, Advaita Ashram, 15th Impression 2004).

As for his equitarian humanism, he not only preached but practiced it himself. In course of his protracted journeys in the country, he kept company even with petty thieves of the most degraded caste and recognized even in highway robbers "sinners who were potential saints". While touring through Central India, he lived with a family of out-caste sweepers. He shared the sufferings and tribulations of the downtrodden castes everywhere and found spiritual treasurers in many of them. Severely pained by their miserable plight, he echoed Swami Rama Krishna's words: "Religion is not for empty belies" and that the first duty of religion is "to care for the poor and to raise them".

Apart from his sparkling spiritualism and commitment to uplift the poor and the downcast, there is a third dimension to Vivekanda's personality which has not been appropriately acknowledged in our Country. That is his ardent and robust nationalism. Our wounded nationalism under centuries of bondage at that time, found most eloquent expression in the outbursts of the Swami from time to time. One of his stirring invocations to India's nationalist spirit was made in his lecture "My plan of campaign" at Madras on his return from America. He thundered: "My India, arise! ... Each nation, like each individual, has one theme in this life, which is its centre, the principal note round which every other comes to form the harmony. If any nation attempts to throw off its national vitality that nation dies. In India religious life forms the centre, the key note of the whole music of the national life. Social reform and politics have to be preached through the vitality of your religion...Every man has to make his own choice; so has every nation. We made our choice ages ago. And it is the faith in the Immortal Soul", that is in the ideology of Vedanta.

Thus Swami Vivekananda was the first real awakener of India's national consciousness. The subsequent nationalist leaders of the Country derived their inspiration, consciously or un-consciously, from the stirring mantra of nationalism taught by the Swami. In fact, Mahatma Gandhi's commitment to the uplift of the poor and the downcast can be traced directly to the messages of Vivekananda and his spiritual mentor Swami Rama Krishna.

But what was the content of his nationalism? Was it his attachment to the mere land mass that forms the Indian sub-continent? Of course, that was it, in the first place, as it had to be naturally. But his nationalism was much more than his love for the geographical entity that is India. It was his unflinching commitment to the basic faith of Vedic religion or Hinduism-faith in the Immortal Soul (Brahman). He made it clear in his very first address to the Parliament of Religions in America, when bowing to Goddess Saraswati, he spoke in the name of the most ancient Vedic religious order, that is Hinduism. And he repeated it when he said that the Hindu Nation had given shelter to religious refugees of other lands in the past.

And again in his written address to the Hindus of Madras "In Defence of Hinduism", he noted that "though whirlwind after whirlwind of foreign invasion has passed over the devoted head of India, though centuries of neglect on our part and contempt on the part of our conquerors have visibly dimmed the glories of ancient Aryavarta,.... the centre is all sound, the keystone is unimpaired." The unmistakable reference here is to the havoc wrought on the ancient Hindu civilization by the Islamist conquerors of India.

He was greatly stung by the criticisms verging on abuses flung by Christian missionaries against Hindus day and night. To them, he said: "If, foreign friends, you come with genuine sympathy to help and not to destroy, god-speed to you. But if by abuses..., you mean only the triumphant assertion of the moral superiority of your own nation, let me tell you plainly, if such a comparison be instituted with any amount of justice, the Hindu will be found head and shoulder above all other nations in the world as a moral race" ("In Defence of Hinduism" by Swami Vivekananda, published by Advaita Ashram, 12th Impression, 1999).

It is thus quite evident from his speeches and writings that he identified India's nationhood with its grand old Hindu civilization. It is this identification of Indianism with Hinduism which Nirad C.Choudhury emphasized when he wrote, as quoted in an earlier chapter, that if Hinduism disappeared at any time, the people of India would cease to have any distinctive identity.

But Vivekananda's Hinduism was not a narrow, bigoted single track religion that denied other faiths. To him, the Hindu religion based upon the teachings of the Vedas was truly Universalist with enough space for followers of other faiths. By Vedas, he did not mean any particular book containing the words of a prophet, but the accumulated treasure of spiritual wisdom of Indian sages and seers since ancient times. He observed: "From the high spiritual flights of the Vedanta philosophy to the low ideas of idolatry with its multifarious mythology, the agnosticism of the Buddhists and the atheism of the Jains, each and all have a place in Hindu religion."

His broad view of Hinduism would accommodate even Islam and Christianity in it if only they agreed. In a letter to a Muslim in June 1898, he even complemented Islam for practising equality in the worship of the universal God in day to day life. He talked of harmonizing the Vedas, the Bible and the Koran and wrote in the letter referred to above:"Mankind ought to be taught that religions are but the varied expressions of the Religion which is oneness, so that each may choose the path that suits him best." What more could be said about the breadth of vision and wide sweep of Hinduism? It is this broad based Universalist Hinduism which Vivekananda refers to when he talks of India's Hindu nationhood.

In this sense, Vivekananda can truly be regarded as the father of Modern Indian nationalism defined by the ancient Hindu civilization. For Hinduism, with its acceptance of diverse modes of worship, is the single most identifying mark of India's nationhood. Apart from the great spiritual height of Vedanta, it is the worship of Shiva, Shakti and Vishnu in their diverse incarnations which unites the common masses from north to south and east to west. It is this Hindu tradition, so well highlighted by Swami Vivekananda, which gives India its national identity. In this sense, India, with its ethos of toleration and acceptance of diverse faiths, can survive only if Hinduism survives. That is the focal point of Swami Vivekananda's concept of Hindu nationalism.

19

Dr. Hedgewar : The pioneer of Nationalist Hinduism

Swami Vivekananda had two-fold mission of identifying religion with service of suffering humanity and inspiring Hindu nationalist awakening in modern India. He sought to achieve the first by founding the Rama Krishna Mission dedicated to the service of suffering humanity. He proclaimed: "where should you go to seek for God? Are not all the poor, the miserable, the weak, good? Why not worship them first?". His Rama Krishna Mission accordingly has come to be associated with humanitarian services like famine relief, maintenance of orphanages, schools and health care centres for the poor.

His second mission of bringing about Hindu nationalist awakening has been well brought out in his lecture "The Mission of the Vedanta". He said: "But this is not the time for us to weep .. We have had weeping enough; no more is this the time for us to become soft. This softness has been with us till we have become like masses of cotton. What our country now wants is muscles of iron and nerves of steel... Why is it that we... have been ruled for the last thousand years by any and every handful of foreigners? Because they had faith in themselves and we had not." That was a clarion call to arouse the spirit of Hindu nationalism rooted in Vedanta - the quintessence of Hinduism.

But his vision of Hindu nationalism got blurred in the welter of confusion surrounding the subsequent nationalist movement for independence. The British imperialists instigated and fully exploited Muslim separatism to stall nationalist struggle for independence. And our tallest nationalist leaders like Bal Gangadhar Tilak and Mahatma Gandhi fell into their trap. It was Tilak who, as leader of the Indian National Congress, signed the infamous Lucknow Pact in 1916 accepting all separatist demands of the Muslim League, fostered and nourished by the British. Grant of separate electorates, weightage and reservations for Muslims irreparably fractured the united Indian nationalism envisaged by Swami Vivekananda.

Mahatma Gandhi went a step further when in 1919 he joined the Khilafat agitation led by the fundamentalist Moulana brothers - Mohammed Ali and Shaukat Ali. This was a disastrous move, for it gave phillip to Muslim separatist solidarity for a fanatical cause which had nothing to do with India. Both Tilak and Gandhi sought to end Muslim separatism, sponsored and sustained by the British, by catering to their separatist agenda, which proved to be counterproductive. Instead of dousing the fire of Muslim separateness, the Lucknow Pact and Khilafat agitation added fuel to it.

Thus Swami Vivekananda's vision of Indian nationalism lay in ruins at the end of the Khilafat fiasco. That was the last straw on the back of Hindu nationalists burning with the flame of patriotism lit by Swami Vivekananda. They could no longer depend on conventional nationalists to carry forward the legacy of the Swami and fulfill his mission of national regeneration. It fell to the lot of a great revolutionary freedom-fighter - Dr.Keshav

Baliram Hedgewar - to take up from where Vivekananda had left and complete his second mission.

Keshav was born at Nagpur on 1st April, 1889 in a family of Brahmin scholars tracing their origin to Ashwalayana Sutra of Rigveda. His father Baliram Pant Hedgewar was well versed in Hindu scriptures and lived off priesthood. At the age of 13, Keshav lost both his parents who died in the epidemic of plague that swept across Nagpur in 1902. But inspite of extreme economic hardship, which meant even going without food sometimes, he carried on with his studies as well as patriotic activism. For his open hostility to the British, he had to change schools from Nagpur to Yeotmal and finally to Pune from where he did his matriculation.

He then came back to Nagpur and got in close contact with revolutionary freedom fighters. Meanwhile, the Nagpur group of revolutionaries had established contact with the revolutionary outfit of Calcutta known as Anusheelan Samiti. They wanted Keshav to move to Calcutta to get in touch with Pulin Bihari Das of Anusheelan Samiti. Accordingly, Keshav Hedgewar came over to Calcutta in 1910 with the ostensible purpose of studying medicine but with the real objective of carrying on with the revolutionary activities.

During the next five years that he stayed in Calcutta pursuing his medical studies, he actively engaged in revolutionary activities as a hard core member of Anusheelan Samiti. And when he returned to Nagpur early in 1916 after doing his medical course, Dr.Keshav Hedgewar plunged headlong in the fight for freedom. He got actively engaged with a revolutionary group called "Kranti Dal" which believed in wresting freedom through armed rebellion. He established contact with underground revolutionaries of Bengal and Punjab in preparation for an armed uprising against the British then engaged in a deadly war.

But the victory of the British in the First World War changed the situation drastically in favour of the Raj. The British set out to crush the revolutionaries and many of them were arrested and tortured. This resulted in great demoralization in the rank of the activists working for armed rebellion. Dr. Hedgewar, however, remained actively engaged with the broad-based national liberation movement led by the Indian National Congress. The Jallianwallabagh massacre spurred him on to carry on the fight against the British with renewed vigour.

As the leader of a volunteer group, he whole-heartedly participated in the Indian National Congress session held in December 1920 at Nagpur—the heartland of revolutionaries. He and his friends even drafted a resolution calling for "complete Independence" for adoption by the Congress, but it was not taken up. Even though he disapproved of Gandhiji mixing up the Khilafat cause with the non-cooperation movement launched in 1921, he jumped into the movement the whole hog. He moved around lighting up the flame of freedom in the hearts of the people. For his fiery speeches delivered at Katol and Bharatwada, he was prosecuted in May 1921 and sent to prison in August 1921.

Dr. Hedgewar was released from prison in July 1922 after undergoing one year's rigorous imprisonment. He was hailed by the nationalists at a grand public reception which was addressed by Congress stalwarts like Pandit Motilal Nehru and Hakim Ajmal Khan who were at Nagpur attending the Congress working committee meeting. But by now, the situation had undergone a sea change. The non-cooperation movement had died down. Gandhiji had finally called it off in the wake of the Chowri Chaura massacre of police men in February 1922. A deep sense of frustration prevailed among freedom fighters who had staked their all in the hope of achieving independence which now seemed as far as ever.

That set Dr.Hedgewar thinking about the status and direction of the national liberation movement. He had noticed that many young people took to patriotic work in a flush of nationalist sentiment but a single blow of suppression by the Colonial regime made them give up the fight. He also took note of the fact that lack of discipline even among genuinely patriotic workers was a great source of weakness. How could such a loose conglomeration of young men take on the well organized might of the imperial government?

What shocked Dr. Hedgewar most was the separatist outlook of Muslim political leadership initiated and fanned by the British. When he asked a fellow Muslim political worker - Sameelullah Khan - why was he wearing a Turkish cap and not a khadi cap which was much in vogue, the Khan replied, "I'm first and foremost a Muslim, and then an Indian". Even Moulana Muhammad AIi, who Gandhiji had almost taken upon his shoulders during the Khilafat agitation, said that he would prefer a degenerate Muslim over a saintly Gandhi.

Dr.Hedgewar was horrified to find that the Khilafat movement supported by the Congress had, instead of integrating the Muslims with the nationalists, had further separated them from the national mainstream. He had earlier argued with Gandhiji against taking up the Khilafat cause apprehending that it would breed extra-territorial religious separatism among the Muslims in India. His worst apprehension had now come true. He had worked with patriotic Muslim friends in close co-operation. He insisted that Muslims should look upon themselves as equals with Hindus and not as 'minorities'. He was clear in his mind that the majority-minority syndrome was a creation of the British to check-mate the growing national liberation movement.

Dr.Hedgewar saw through the British game plan and decided to counter it in his own way. If under British instigation,

Muslim politics remained separatist, there was no other way than to organize the Hindus to carry on with the freedom struggle on their own. In any case, Hindus, who constituted over 80% of India's population, formed the core of India's nationhood. He concluded that if the perpetuation of British rule through the politics of Muslim separatism had to be challenged Hindu people had to be organized into a disciplined force imbued with intense spirit of nationalism.

He remembered Swami Vivekananda's words that the people of India (obviously referring to Hindus) had become soft like "mass of cotton" and needed to develop "muscles of iron and nerves of steel". And decided to give shape to Vivekananda's unfulfilled mission of building up Hindu nationalism. With this end in view and the goal of India's independence upper most in his mind, Dr. Hedgewar took a momentous decision. It was the decision to establish a cadre of young men involved with the sublime values of the great Hindu civilization dedicated to the cause of India's true national regeneration. That led to the birth of the Rashtriya Swayam-Sewak Sangh (RSS) in October 1925. More of it in the next Chapter.

20

Dr. Hedgewar, the Great Nationalist Institution - Builder

The political scenario in 1924-25 was depressing from the point of view of freedom-fighters. Gandhiji's non-cooperation movement, which had aroused so much hope among the people, had faded away. And freedom was nowhere in sight. In the circumstances, Dr. Hedgewar realized that there was no short-cut to freedom and the struggle for it was going to be a long drawn out affair. It called for a lot of effort at organizing and preparing.

He recalled Swami Vivekananda's observation that lack of organizing spirit was a big short-coming of Hindu character. If Hindus had to be the lead force in the fight for freedom, they had to be effectively organized on a lasting basis. Swami Vivekanand had also deplored the physical weakness of Hindu youths and their lack of faith in themselves and their civilisational heritage. Following in the footsteps of the Swami, Dr. Hedgewar decided to remedy this weakness of Hindu Youth also in his own way.

It was in this background, with the inspiring message of Swami Vivekananda uppermost in his mind, that the idea of establishing a national volunteer organization dedicated to India's freedom and national regeneration took shape in Dr.Hedgewar's mind. Accordingly, he collected a few committed young men at his house in Nagpur on Vijaya Dashmi day in 1925 and founded the Rashtriya Swayamsevak Sangh (RSS). Inaugurating the Sangh, he observed; "All of us must train ourselves physically, intellectually and in every way so as to be capable of achieving our cherished goal".

Once he took the historic step of founding the Sangh, Dr. Hedgewar never looked back. He nourished the sapling of the Sangh planted at Nagpur with his sweat until it grew into a gigantic tree of nationalist idealism with its twigs and branches spread over the whole country. He concentrated the entire energy of his dynamic personality in building up the Sangh as a potent instrument of individual character building and national resurgence. He thus committed his life now to a mission which was far higher than mere political.

And yet, while guiding the Sangh to emerge as a lead organization of true national resurgence, he never ceased to be a part of the struggle for independence. He continued to be actively associated with freedom movement led by the Indian National Congress. As a working committee member of the Central Provinces Congress, he attended its Calcutta session towards the end of 1928. On this occasion, he had a long talk with Subhash Chandra Bose about his plan of action. Being highly impressed, Subhash Bose is reported to have said: "There is no doubt that yours is the only effective method of emancipating the nation".

At its Lahore session in December 1929, the Congress under the presidentship of Jawahar Lal Nehru declared "Purna Swaraj" (complete independence) as its goal. It fixed 26 January,

1930 for public affirmation of independence pledge. This sent the patriotic spirit of Dr. Hedgewar soaring high and he promptly directed all Shakhas of the Sangh to celebrate 26th January 1930 as Independence Day. In his letter to the Shakhas, he said, "We of the Sangh are naturally immensely happy that the All India Congress has endorsed our goal of complete independence".

In the same spirit, he heartily welcomed Gandhiji's move to launch the Salt Satyagraha in April 1930. He was totally committed to any movement to weaken and demolish the British Raj. He encouraged the Sangh members to join the Satyagraha. And more. He decided to participate in the Satyagraha himself in his own way on his own turf. In July 1930, Dr. Hedgewar alongwith his band of Satyagrahis broke the Jungle Law by entering the prohibited reserve forest near Pusad. He was arrested, prosecuted and sentenced to 9 months imprisonment.

By the time he came out of prison in February 1931, Dr.Hedgewar was gravely concerned about the deepening unholy alliance between the British imperialists and Muslim separatists. For in the Round Table Conference in 1931, Muslim separatist leaders had openly come out in support of the British rulers against the nationalist demands for freedom. At a meeting in the House of Commons in 1932, the Agha Khan, Allama Iqbal and historian Shafaat Ahmed Khan proclaimed "the inherent impossibility of securing any merger of Hindu and Muslim political or indeed social interests". What was more shocking, they went to the extent of asserting "the impracticality of ever governing India through anything but a British agency".

As a reward, the British rulers announced the notorious "Communal Award" in 1932 conceding all separatist demands of Muslim Communalists. These included separation of Sindh from Bombay to make it a Muslim majority province, 33 1/2 per cent reservation for Muslims in Central legislature, continuation of separate electorate etc. Dr. Hedgewar was the only nationalist leader who boldly and openly warned that the poison of separatism injected into the body politic would ultimately lead to partition of the country. But the mainstream political leadership paid no heed to his far-sighted warning which proved to be prophetic. The Congress meekly succumbed to the British game plan by refusing to reject the infamous Award outright.

Dr. Hedgewar realized that the Communal Award was the Magna Carta of Muslim separatism granted by the wily British to ward off the freedom movement. It confirmed his belief that only a strong nationalist surge based on Hindu consolidation could humble the British power and achieve freedom. That alone would convince the Muslims that their interest lay in merging with the nationalist mainstream rather than siding with the British. Accordingly, he proceeded with renewed vigor to strengthen the Sangh and widen its spread in different parts of the country.

It is not generally known that Mahatma Gandhi himself visited the Wardha district camp of the Sangh on 25 December 1934. Being impressed by the activities of the Sangh, Gandhiji is reported to have remarked, "Doctorji, your organization is admirable. I am aware of the fact that you were for many years a Congress worker. Why did you not build such a Volunteer Cadre under a popular organization like the Congress itself?". At the end of the visit, Gandhiji is reported to have remarked; "Doctorji, with your character and sincerity, there is no doubt you will succeed".

Even as Gandhiji continued to harp on Hindu-Muslim unity as a pre-condition for achieving freedom, the canker of Muslim separatism kept growing to menacing proportions. In July 1935, C. Rahmat Ali issued a statement in Cambridge supporting the demand for Pakistan comprising Muslim Majority Provinces of India. Dr.Hedgewar was confirmed that chasing

Hindu Muslim unity before achievement of freedom was like putting the cart before the horse. He therefore opted for freedom first and decided to go the whole hog for it.

It may be noted that Gandhiji himself came round to this view when he launched the "Quit India" movement in August 1942 even as the Muslim separatists were opposed to it. The crowning slogan of the 1942 movement was that the British should go first and Hindu-Muslim unity would follow. This was exactly what Dr.Hedgewar had believed in and acted upon earlier.

Dr.Hedgewar's total commitment to achievement of freedom and his great organizing capacity drew the attention of Subhas Chandra Bose. Bose had broken away from Congress and formed his Forward Block to launch the final assault on the British. Towards this end, he was scheduled to meet Dr. Hedgewar at Bombay in July 1939. But the meeting could not take place because Dr. Hedgewar was not in a position to move to Bombay due to ill health.

Even as he was hovering between bouts of serious illness and partial recovery, Dr. Hedgewar's passion for India's freedom became more and more intense. While staying at Rajgir (Bihar) in March-April 1940 for rest and recoupment, he was heard uttering: "Oh, look there! The year 1940 is already passing. And yet we have achieved nothing; We continue to be a subject nation. But some day, we shall attain freedom". Freedom, his highest aspiration for which he struggled all through his life, did come, but not in his life time.

Towards the end of his illustrious life, Subhas Bose came over to Nagpur to meet Dr.Hedgewar on 20 June 1940. But meeting of the two great freedom fighters could not take place because Dr. Hedgewar was on his death-bed at the time. He passed away the very next morning on 21 June 1940 at the relatively young age of 51 years. But not before establishing the R.S.S. as a stout nationalist organization to sustain the grand Hindu civilization through the stormy times to come.

It speaks volumes about their achievements that the three greatest redeemers of the time-honored Hindu Civilization - Adi Shankaracharya, Vivekananda and Dr. Hedgewar - had rather short life-span. They all died relatively young - Adi Shankaracharya at the age of 32, Swami Vivekananda at 39 and Dr. Hedgewar at 51. And yet, each of them did so much to keep the universalist all- inclusive Hindu Civilization live through difficult times as no other single individual has done.

21

Sri Guruji (M.S. Golwalkar) : Reincarnation of Swami Vivekananda

After Dr. Hedgewar, the mantle of the Sangh came upon Sri Madhav Sadashiv Golwalkar, respectfully referred to as Sri Guruji by his innumerable followers and admirers. Not because he came to head the Sangh, but for other reasons which shall be dealt with a little later.

As it happened, Dr. Hedgewar the founder of the Sangh, bequeathed to Sri. M.S. Golwalkar the onus of heading the R.S.S. as its Sar-Sanghchalak on the eve of his death in June 1940. On the face of it, the decision might appear surprising. Dr. Hedgewar founded the Sangh in 1925. He had a number of senior associates with him since its inception, one of whom could legitimately succeed him as head of the Sangh. One of them - Appaji Joshi - was particularly close to Dr. Hedgewar and considered to be his right hand. On the other hand, Sri Golwalkar, 16-17 years junior to him in age, was a relatively recent entrant into the Sangh fold. Although he started taking interest in the activities of the

Sangh since around 1933, Sri Golwalkar was formally initiated as a Swayang Sewak only around the first quarter of 1938. (Significantly, he was administered oath as a Sangh volunteer by Dr. Hedgewar himself in his own house).

Even otherwise, there was little in common between Dr. Hedgewar and Sri Golwalkar in regard to their initial orientation and leanings. Dr. Hedgewar was a hard-boiled revolutionary freedom-fighter right from his youthful years coming out in the open on every conceivable occasion. Sri Golwalker, on the other hand, was inclined towards spiritual pursuits in his student days. He started the practice of evening prayers and morning "Surya Namaskar" from the time he entered school after his primary education at home. And, while at Varanasi for his university education at B.H.U., he spent his spare time in quiet contemplation and meditation. At this stage while Dr.Hedgewar was attracted to the Anusheelan Samity - the revolutionary outfit of Bengal, Sri Golwalkar was drawn towards the Ram Krishna Mission established by Swami Vivekananda.

In this background, when one thinks of Dr. Hedgewar, one thinks of revolutionary freedom-fighters like V.D. Sawarkar and Netaji Subhash Chandra Bose. But when one thinks of Sri Golwalkar, one thinks of saints like Swami Vivekananda and Adi Sankaracharya. And yet, it is a tribute to the vision and far sight of Dr. Hedgewar that he chose Sri Golwalkar to succeed him as the head of the Sangh. And Sri Guruji, as addressed by all, steered the organization for 33 long years through most difficult times from 1940 to 1973.

A brief profile of Sri Guruji would be in place here. Born on 19th February 1906 at Nagpur, Madhav Sadashiv Golwalkar was the only surviving son among nine children of his parents. His father, Sadashiv Rao was a school teacher who kept moving from place to place on routine transfers until he settled down in Ramtek after retirement. He subsequently shifted to Nagpur around 1942 which came to be his final resting place. The boy Madhav started his school education in 1915 and passed the matric examination in 1922. After doing his ISC from Hislop College, Nagpur, he entered Benaras Hindu University from where he got his Master's degree in Science (M.Sc.) in 1928.

It was during his university education at Varanasi that Sri Golwalkar got interested in the Hindu cause under the magnetic impact of Sri Madan Mohan Malviya, the veteran Hindu nationalist leader and founder of the B.H.U. But his interest was focused on study of Hindu scriptures along with academic studies in which he always excelled. He was equally interested in outdoor activities, much like Swami Vivekananda in his early student days, and played hockey and tennis. From August 1931 to the end of 1932, he also worked as a demonstrator in the Zoology department of B.H.U.

He returned to Nagpur early in 1933 and, at the insistence of his mother, started study of law to do his L.L.B which he completed in 1935. Even during this period, he studied important religious books like "Advait Sidhi" and "Panchadashi" and became well versed in Advait Vedanta dwelt upon by Adi Shankaracharya and Swami Vivekananda. In fact, he had studied the entire literature of Rama Krishna Paramahans and Swami Vivekanand while at Varanasi itself and continued his link with Rama Krishna Mission whenever he came to Nagpur. He served in B.H.U. as a professor for a couple of years which earned him the affectionate name of "Guruji" from his students who adored him for his saintly attribute an affection for them. This reverential surname or title given to him by his students at B.H.U. stuck to him all through his life.

From 1933 onwards, whenever Sri Guruji was in Nagpur during vacations in B.H.U. he used to meet Dr. Hedgewar and started coming under his magnetic influence. At the same time, he made it a point to visit the Rama Krishna Ashram at Nagpur.

Thus started his close association with the two epoc making organizations - the Rama Krishna Mission started by Swami Vivekananda in 1897 and R.S.S. founded by Dr. Hedgewar in 1925 - which moulded his entire life and merged into his dynamic personality.

At this stage, Sri Guruji's inner urge was primarily towards spiritual pursuits which drew him more and more towards Rama Krishna Mission. So much so that one fine morning towards the end of October or early November, 1936, he quietly left Nagpur for Saragachhi Ashram of Rama Krishna Math in North Bengal close to the Himalayas to become a "Sanyasi". He made his first move to take to a life of asceticism to the utter surprise of everyone at Nagpur, including his beloved parents who were looking forward to his settling down at Nagpur as a lawyer. It was very much like Narendra (Swami Vivekananda) who had left his spiritual home at Baranagore in July 1890 to take retreat in the Himalayas for spiritual contemplation initially.

Swami Akhandananda, a Gurubhai of Swami Vivekananda, was the head of Rama Krishna Mission at Saragachhi. He took Madhav Rao (Sri Guruji) under his wings on his arrival at Saragachhi and was highly impressed by his devotion and commitment. Being old and sick, Swamiji was in the last leg of his life at that time and Sri Guruji left no stone unturned to serve him and keep him going. Recognizing his deep spiritual urge, Swami Akhandananda personally initiated Sri Guruji into the Rama Krishna Mission order of "Sanyasis" in a simple ceremony on 13th January 1937. After the anniversary of Swami Vivekananda's birth on 2 February 1937), the Swami was shifted to Calcutta on the night of 6 February for his ultimate medical treatment and passed away in the afternoon of 7 February 1937. Sri Guruji was with him till his last hour. In his last days, the Swamiji is reported to have asked him to go out and serve the society at large.

It would be interesting to speculate what course Sri Guruji would have adopted if Swami Akhandananda had lived longer. He was so deeply attached to Swami Vivekananda that one cannot conceive of his detaching himself from Rama Krishna Mission during Akhandananda's life - time. But that would be a futile exercise in the realm of speculative imagination. As it turned out, destiny had willed a much bigger role for him in preservation and sustenance of the great Hindu civilization from outside the confines of the Ashram. But the basic spirit of "Sanyas" he had imbibed in course of his association with Rama Krishna Mission remained with him all through his life. In his subsequent avatar as the leading light of the Sangh, he was truly a Sanyasi in action, a seer engaged in "Karma Yog" in pursuance of "Yug Dharma".

After Swami Akhandananda's passing away, Sri Guruji returned to Nagpur as suddenly as he had earlier departed for Saragachhi. The Swami's death seemed to have left a deep impact on him and he kept himself largely confined to his studies in quiet isolation. Till the end of the year 1937, Sri Guruji kept to himself in quiet contemplation - possibly thinking about his future course. And then one fine morning in the beginning of the year 1938, he proceeded to the local R.S.S. Shakha and participated in the drill as a Swayangsewak. His mind had been made up. He committed himself to the Sangh and dedicated his life to it. It was at this stage that he was formally enrolled or initiated into the Sangh personally by Dr.Hedgewar. And once he took to the Sangh, he never looked back till his last breath.

Dr. Hedgewar had an eye on him since 1933 when Sri Guruji started taking interest in Sangh activities, though not yet enrolled in its rank. He was elated at the thought of the such a highly educated university teacher being involved with the Sangh and started paying special attention to him. Sri Bhaiyajee Dani, who later rose to be the Principal Secretary of the Sangh, acted as a link between Dr.Hedgewar and Sri Guruji.

Through his effort, there used to be close interaction between Dr. Hedgewar and Sri Guruji whenever the latter came to Nagpur from Varanasi during university holidays.

In fact, Dr. Hedgewar had felt disappointed when Sri Guruji suddenly left Nagpur for Sargachhi in pursuit of his deep spiritual urge. He was therefore naturally very happy when Sri Guruji returned back to Nagpur, and more so when he formally joined the Sangh in early 1938. Thereafter, he started taking Sri Guruji with him in all important meetings of the Sangh. When the ailing Dr. Hedgewar moved from Nagpur to Nasik and then to Deolali, Sri Guruji stuck to him like a shadow and served him with the same devotion as he had served the ailing Swami Akhandanand earlier.

Dr. Hedgewar recovered a bit and returned to Nagpur, but he knew that he was nearing his end. Accordingly, he installed Sri Guruji as the Principal Secretary (Sarkaryawah) of the Sangh in August 1939 and started sharing his onerous burden of work with him. He had earlier sounded his associates and prominent Sangh activists about the choice of Sri Guruji as the future head of the organization and obtained their enthusiastic support. And just a day before his death in June 1940, the gravely ailing Dr. Hedgewar called his chief associates and told Sri Guruji in their presence to take the responsibility of the Sangh after him. Accordingly, Sri M.S. Golwalkar or Sri Guruji was formally installed as the second Sar Sanghchalak of R.S.S. early in July 1940.

It was an awesome responsibility thrust upon the young shoulders of this saintly scholar-cum-social activist at one of the most critical junctures of India's recent history. How he coped with it with 'the nerve of steel', as desired by Swami Vivekananda, is part of another story to be dealt with in the next chapter.

22

The Helmsman Sar Sanghchalak of the Sangh in Turbulent Times

It would have been a tough assignment at any time. To steer the ship of the sangh through the rough and turbulent waters of 1940's was an extremely difficult task. More so when the helmsman happened to be as raw and new to the job as Sri Guruji at the young age of 34. It is a true measure of his greatness that the sangh not only survived through the deadly blows administered to it during the period, but eventually emerged as the biggest social organization in the country.

The first blow on the Sangh was administered by the British rulers within months of Sri Guruji's installation as Sar Sangh Chalak. In August 1940, the colonial administration imposed a ban on the use of Khaki uniform and lathi drill by R.S.S.s Volunteers under the draconian Defence of India Rules then in force in the backdrop of the world war. Since the Sangh was known to be a committed patriotic organization, it was a thorn in the flesh of the foreign rulers who were ever eager to crush it on one pretext or another. The ban order would have crippled the Sangh under a weak leadership, but Sri Guruji was made of a different stuff. He nullified the prohibition order by replacing the Khaki Shirt with white shirt and lathi with 'lejhim' (a kind of elongated musical instrument) to be used by Swangsewaks for the Shakha drill. For the essence of the Shakha technique was to inculcate the spirit of brotherhood, devotion to the mother land, selfless service, discipline and physical fitness among the volunteers, and not to train them in the use of arms.

The R.S.S. it must be remembered, was not meant to produce a cadre of armed men, as often alleged by its critics, but aimed at character-building among the youth dedicated to the cause of the nation. Sri Golwalkar saw to it that the organization stuck to the path of national resurgence without deviating into any futile adventurism or bravado. The need of the hour was to motivate the volunteers to be ready for any sacrifice in the fight for freedom which had reached a critical stage.

By early 1942, the defining moment had arrived for India's struggle for independence. The British rulers were in a tight corner being engaged in a grim world war in which they were at the receiving end. Communist Russia had allied with the British in the war after Nazi Germany attacked it and made considerable advance in Russian territory. True to their extra-territorial loyalty, the Indian communists had become friends with the British. The Muslim League under Jinnah's leadership had passed the resolution for creation of Pakistan and the Muslims in India had rallied behind the League. They were dead opposed to grant of independence without Pakistan, which was not acceptable to the nationalist forces led by the Indian National Congress. In such a background, the nationalist forces were getting impatient to launch the final assault to extort freedom from the British even without the Muslims and communists.

The situation was getting ripe for taking initiative to seize power from the British for another reason also. The lightening Japanese advance in South East Asia had made the position of the British rulers in India highly vulnerable and suspect. Japan had captured Burma in March 1942 and the British had ingloriously exited from there leaving the Burmese people at the mercy of the Japanese conquerors. The nationalists in India perceived of a similar danger of the British leaving the Indian people to fend for themselves in case of Japanese advance into India. It was all the more necessary, therefore, to wrest power from the tottering British empire in time to be in a position to resist the Japanese with all the might of aroused Indian nationalism.

In this sombre backdrop, Sri Guruji held a meeting of some selected Sangh functionaries at the residence of Sri Bhaurao Abhyankar at Poona (Pune) in May 1942. He made a through analysis of the national and international satiation as described above, and observed: "In the near future wherever there is opportunity, the British rule should be uprooted and power should be taken in our own hands". Later, addressing the Swayamsewaks in the evening, he told them to be ready to sacrifice their lives in the sacred war of freedom.

That was in May 1942. Subsequent events amply proved that Sri Golwalkar was thinking exactly on the same lines as Mahatma Gandhi at that time. For only a few months later, Gandhiji launched the famous 'Quit India' movement against the British in August 1942 which shock the whole country as well as the foundations of the British Empire. What followed is history. The Sangh Volunteers took active part in the 'Quit India' movement as true patriots wherever they were in a position to do so in their personal capacity, even as the Muslims in general kept aloof and communists were positively hostile to it. It is no mere coincidence that the maximum impact of 1942 August Revolution was felt in Maharashtra which was also the stronghold of the Sangh. In fact Satara near Pune was one of the few places in the country which was fully liberated for some time during that period. With the blessings of Sri Golwalkar, the Sangh Volunteers provided safe shelter to many of the prominent revolutionaries who went underground after the sweeping crack-down by the colonial regime against the freedom fighters. In that period, the underground revolutionaries considered the house of any Sangh Volunteer as a safe haven and made full use of it to carry forward their revolutionary activities.

Some of the notable revolutionary freedom fighters who took shelter with Sangh activists were Smt. Aruna Asaf Ali with Lala Hans Raj Gupta, Achyut Patwardhan with Bhau Saheb Deshmukh, Sane Guruji with Moti Lal Apte, to name only a few. There were numerous other freedom-fighters who were similarly sheltered by R.S.S. men in other parts of the country. At the same time, Sri Golwalkar made sure that the apolitical character of the Sangh as a basically social organization was maintained in the long-term interest of society and the country. He didn't commit the Sangh as a body to the movement for the simple reason that it was not a political organization, but a social force with broad nation-building perspective.

And yet, the Sangh didn't flinch from contributing its mite to the national cause whenever the occasion demanded it. When the process of transfer of power began at the end of the war in 1945, the most important issue was the territorial unity of India after the departure of the British. The Muslim League, with the tacit support of the British, was hellben on securing Pakistan by partitioning the country, which was being stoutly opposed by the nationalist forces all over the country. Mahatma Gandhi had pronounced to sacrifice his life to prevent what he called the "vivisection of India" . Sri Golwalkar lent his full force to the campaign against partition of the country. He moved tirelessly around the country arousing the people against the move of partition and preparing the Sangh cadres for any sacrifice to preserve the unity and integrity of India.

But when partition became a reality in 1947, under circumstances which are well known, Sri Golwalkar had only two options. Being a Sanyasi by instinct, he could have retreated to the Himalayas and become a Yogi, like Sri Aurobindo earlier. The other option was to face the reality and minimize the pangs of partition. Being a true karmayogi, Sri Golwalkar chose the latter course. That was also in accordance with the advice he had received from Swami Akhandanand to go out and serve the society.

It was a frightful and heart-breaking situation which Sri Golwalkar and the Sangh had to reckon with in the run up to the eventual partition. The whole of what is Pakistan now, that is West Punjab, Northwest Frontier and Sindh, was going through a virtual genocide of Hindus and Sikhs at the hands of fanatic Muslim hordes instigated by the Muslim League. What happened in Kahuta, a prosperous village in west Punjab in early 1947, provides a glimpse into the dark scenario of that period. In their famous book, *Freedom at Midnight*", Larry Collins and Dominique Lapiare describe: " a Moslem horde had descended on the village like wolf pack, setting fire to the houses in its Sikh and Hindu quarters with buckets of gasoline. In minutes, the area was engulfed in fire and entire families, screaming pitifully for help, were consumed by the flames. Those who escaped were caught, tied together, soaked with gasoline and burned alive... ... ...A few Hindu women hauled from their beds to be raped and converted to Islam, survived, others had broken away from their captors and hurled themselves back into the fire to perish with their families."

That was in preparation for the birth of Pakistan (The Land of the pure cleansed of Hindus and Sikhs). The mayhem against Hindus and Sikhs continued with greater ferocity after the birth of Pakistan in August 1947, resulting in wholesale the migration of Hindus and Sikhs from there. A placard displayed on a refugee train that arrived from Pak territory with corpses and mutilated bodies of Hindus and Sikhs in September 1947 read "Pakistan Ka Tohfa (gift from Pakistan)".

In such a grim situation, Sri Golwalkar mobilized the Sangh workers in West Punjab and Sindh to go all out to protect the beleaguered Hindus and Sikhs in Pakistan and assist in their safe passage into India. That was the supreme task to which the Sangh workers in Pak territory addressed themselves at great risk to their own lives. In the process, thousands of them perished at the hands of the Pak marauders, but they had succeeded in saving the lives of lacs of Hindus and Sikhs and ensuring their safe transit to India.

Retaliatory violence against Muslims in the Indian part of Punjab had made the situation truly grim. Massacre of their kith and kin in Pakistani Punjab had provoked the Hindus and Sikhs of Indian Punjab to explode against Muslims in their areas. The gravity of the situation is well brought out in the day to day diary of Alan Campbell Johnson, a staff member of the viceroy Lord Mountbatten, in the immediate aftermath of the partition. He records" "16th August 1947. Even as we met, momentous news was coming in from both the partitioned provinces... .. .. In the Punjab the people are taking the situation into their own hands.

"27th August 1947, Mountbatten then turned to a general account of what was happening in Punjab. The Sikhs, he said had launched an attack... ... .. they were adamant and had in fact observed that they were waiting for us to go. The situation was now out of their control."

In this explosive backdrop, the disciplined cadres of the Sangh not only kept their calm but saw to it that retaliatory violence did not spread in other parts of the country, where they had a significant presence. For the primary concern of Sri Golwalkar at this critical hour, apart from protecting the Hindus and Sikhs trapped in the Pak Territory, was to prevent the whole of India from being plunged into a dreadful civil war. Sri Golwalkar put the entire weight of his dynamic and sobering personality to prevent such eventuality which would have torn the country apart.

At one stage the national capital Delhi itself, which had a sizeable Muslim population, was seriously threatened by large scale rioting and violence. In their book referred to earlier, Larry Collins and Dominique Lapiarre write that the situation in Delhi was so grave that both Nehru and Patel, the Prime Minister and Home Minister, told Lord Mountbatten, the Governor General, to take command and handle the situation directly. This was based on their interview of Mountbatten later in course of writing of their book. This may or may not be true, but it is well known that Sardar Patel had sought the help and co-operation of Sri Golwalkar and the Sangh Cadres in restoring calm in the riot torn capital and Sri Golwalkar had readily responded to this call. Under his guidance, the Sangh Cadres devoted themselves whole-heartedly in not only protecting Hindus against Muslim aggression but also protecting Delhi from being torn as under by internecine civil strife.

Even earlier before partition, once when Pt. Nehru was to address a rally in Hyderabad (Sindh), now in Pakistan, in 1946 amidst fear of attack by Muslim League hordes, the local Congress leaders had sought the help of Sangh cadres to counter the threat. The local Sangh volunteers then came to their rescue and ensured that Nehru's public meeting was not disturbed.

The most important task in the wake of the partition was the rehabilitation of lacs of Hindus and Sikhs who had to abandon their hearth and home in Pakistan and seek refuge in India. Under Sri Golwalkar's leadership, the Sangh rendered Yeomen's service wiping their tears and helping in their relief and rehabilitation in every possible way. The anguish and anger of Sangh Cadres and Hindu masses against the atrocities committed on their brothers and sisters in Pakistan was thus canalized into constructive channels. Apart from healing the wounds of the refugees, Sri Golwalkar's chief concern was to douse the flame of large scale retaliatory violence against Muslims in India. For a Sanyasi like him, steeped in the Hindu tradition of tolerance and humanism, the very idea of counter-violence against Muslims was totally unacceptable. If the Hindu masses by and large remained calm and peace was maintained in India after religious cleansing in Pakistan, the contribution of Sri Golwalkar and the Sangh was no less than that of other acknowledged leaders of the country.

23

Sri Golwalkar's Test of Fire

The stellar role played by the Sangh Cadres in relief and rehabilitation of the hapless refugees from west and east Pakistan (now Bangladesh) endeared them to the people of the country. The silent service rendered by them without seeking any publicity like professional politicians made them all the more trust worthy and popular among the common man. Sri Golwalkar was greeted by thousands wherever he went, specially in Punjab and other parts of Northern and Western India. And every-where he exhorted the people to keep their calm and work towards stabilization of our new found independence instead of reacting violently to the happenings in Pakistan. Since Hindus, in the wider sense of the term, constituted the backbone of India's nationhood, specially after the creation of Pakistan, he stressed upon consolidation of the Hindu society in the overall interest of the nation.

Towards that end, he committed the Sangh to healing the wounds and wiping the tears of the refugees pouring in from Pakistan. Significantly enough, Mahatma Gandhi, whose highest ambition was to wipe every tear from every human eye in the world, was himself planning to visit Pakistan to restore Hindus and Sikhs in their homes. Referring to Gandhiji, the veteran journalist Durga Das writes that "he told me one day that he had decided to visit Pakistan accompanied by General Shah Nawz Khan of the I.N.A. They had planned to leave in mid - February (1948). He wanted the Hindus and Sikhs and Muslims restored to their homes". ('India: From Curzon To Nehru & After' - by Durga Das). Gandhiji and Golwalkar thus shared a common concern to wipe the tears of Hindus and Sikhs of Pakistan in the immediate aftermath of partition.

Precisely at this moment, came the bolt from the blue, both for the country and the Sangh. In the black afternoon of 30 January 1948, the Mahatma fell to assassin's bullets while at his prayer meeting in Delhi. As it turned out, the dark deed was perpetrated by the satanic threesome - Nathu Ram Godse who fired the shots, Madan Lal Pahwa who backed him up and Gopal Godse who was a part of the heinous conspiracy. Madan Lal Pahwa was an uprooted refugee from Sindh whose family, hearth and home had been destroyed in Pakistan. Nathu Ram and Gopal Godse were perverted extremists. Their black act left the entire nation stunned. The country sunk into darkness.

At that dark hour, Sri Golwalkar was in the midst of a meeting of social activists at Madras in course of his tour of Tamilnadu. The news of the tragedy shattered him beyond measure. He instantly cancelled all his programmes and left for Nagpur to observe thirteen days of mourning. And ironically enough, Sri Golwalkar himself came under the firing line of the ruling politicians who sought to implicate the Sangh in the ghastly crime without any basis whatsoever. It was kind of a blank shot fired by the political establishment with two obvious objectives. First, it helped in diverting the attention of the people from the security lapses which led to the tragedy. And secondly, it was aimed at checking the growing popularity of the Sangh among the people which was worrying the entire political spectrum, even though the Sangh was not a political outfit.

The catastrophe of the Mahatma's murder came as a double tragedy for Sri Golwalkar and the Sangh on account of the perverted perception of the political establishment. It need not and should not have been so. In a way, it was a malignant symptom of the troubled times that followed the end of colonial rule in the whole of South Asia. The topmost leader of every country in South Asia which gained independence after British withdrawal fell victim to assassin's bullets at one time or the other. But nowhere a thoroughly patriotic socio- political organization with impeccable service record like the Sangh was sought to be made the sacrificial goat by the ruling dispensation as in India.

The first lethal shot was fired at the legendry Burmese leader, Aung San, who led the nationalist stuggle for his country's freedom. He was the foremost among the "Thirty Heroes" who, after initially helping the Japanese to oust the British, led the Burmese struggle to liberate the country from the Japanese under the banner of the Anti-Fascist Peoples Freedom League (AFPFL). Even as the process of constitution -making for fully independent Burma was on, Aung San and six other members of the Interim Government of Burma were shot dead while engaged in a cabinet meeting on 19 July 1947. (Incidentally, Ms. Aung San Suukyi, the most visible symbol of pro-democracy movement in Burma, is none other than the daughter of the assassinated leader Aung San.) Agents of the opposition groups led by U. Saw were generally blamed for the killing but there was no witch-hunting of political rivals.

The other towering South Asian leader to fall a victim to assassin's bullets was Prime Minister Liaquat Ali Khan of

Pakistan. After the passing away of M.A. Jinnah in September 1948, Liaquat Ali Khan was the topmost leader of the country who came to be called the Quide-e-Millat. He was shot dead while addressing a public meeting at Rawal Pindi on 16th October 1951. In this case also, some of his cabinet Ministers were vaguely suspected of plotting the killing but there was no effort at implicating any group or individual in the dastardly crime

In neighboring Sri Lanka, S.W.R.D. Bandarnaike emerged as the first charismatic mass leader when his party was swept to power in 1956 on the crest of a Sinhalese cultural, religious (Buddhist) and linguistic upsurge. As a popular leader of the Sinhalese Buddhist masses, he went about regularizing the affairs of Buddhist religious institutions. And precisely at his moment of glory, he was shot deed in September 1959 by a Sinhalese Buddhist monk who had been given an opportunity to place his grievances before him. And yet there was no question of any blanket and blind action against Buddhist order of Monks or organizations in the wake of Bandaranaike's assassination.

But here in India, after the Mahatma's assassination, the Congress party government blindly targeted the Sangh with the twin objective of diverting public attention from its own failure to protect him and tarnishing the image of the most authentic nationalist organization with a Hindu base. There was considerable partisan pressure on the government of the day from even before the tragic event to crush the Sangh for narrow political considerations. This is borne out by a speech delivered by Sardar Patel about the Sangh at Lucknow early in January 1948. He had then observed: "You cannot crush an organization by using the 'danda'. After all, the R.S.S. men are not thieves and dacoits. They are patriots who love their country". ('The Hindu" Madras dated 7 January 1948). In this background, Gandhiji's death at the hands of a Hindu extremist came in handy for the Government to 'crush' the Sangh. The

R.S.S. was promptly banned on 4 February 1948, only four days after the assassination, without even a semblance of evidence to connect the organization with the event.

What was more astounding, even preposterous, was that Sri Golwalkar himself was arrested at Nagpur the very next night on 5th February 1948 on the charge of conspiracy to the killing. That was an eloquent testimony to the malafide or evil intention of the government of the day. There was not an iota of evidence to connect Sri Golwalkar or even the Sangh to the Mahatma's murder, which the Home Ministry discovered shortly after the arrest. This is evident from a letter written by the Home Minister Sardar Patel to Prime Minister Nehru on 27 February 1948. (Sardar Patel's correspondence 1945-50; volume VI, edited by Durga Das, Navajivan Publishing House, Ahmedabad).

Having failed to bring up any charge against Sri Golwalkar, the government had to release him on 6 August 1948, but he was re-arrested on 12 November 1948 for heading a banned organization. For, the ban on the Sangh continued. After recovering from the initial shock at the national tragedy, the Sangh revived to offer Passive resistance or "SATYAGRAHA" against the unjustified ban imposed upon it. Between 11 December 1948 when the "SATYAGRAHA" started and 21st January 1949 when it was called off, thousands of R.S.S. men courted arrest and filled the jails in different parts of the country. Eventually the dark chapter of maligning the Sangh for no fault of its own came to an end as it had to, on 12th July1949 when the ban on it was lifted.

The very next day on 13th July 1949, Sri Golwalkar was released from prison at Baitul and returned to Nagpur amidst tumultuous welcome. The train that brought him to Nagpur was stopped by huge crowds at intermediate railway stations and tens of thousands greeted him on arrival at Nagpur with cries of "BHARAT MATA KI JAI". Emotions ran high and his popularity soared to the skies. He had come up as a shining star after the test of fire. He left the dark chapter behind and set upon revitalizing the Sangh by undertaking a tour of the country from one end to the other. He received thunderous ovation by massive crowds wherever he went. Reporting on the huge public rally he addressed at Delhi's Ramleela Maidan in August 1949, the B.B.C's Delhi correspondent observed: "Sri Golwalkar is a rising and shining star on India's horizon. Today the crowd that he attracts in India can be equalled by none other than Nehru alone."

The most remarkable aspect of Sri Golwalkar's pronouncements hereafter was that there was no trace of anger or bitterness in them against the government of the day. Any other leader or outfit would have reacted differently to the harsh and unjust treatment meted out to them by the country's political establishment. But being a 'Sanyasi' by instinct and patriot by inclination, he remained gracefully unaffected by the unfortunate events of the past. He explained it once during his visit to Umred in Vidarbha in early August 1949. He observed: "The assault on the Sangh by banning it had been made by our own government. Hence we suffered it with utmost restraint. If a foreigner's administration had done it, it would have been made fully acquainted with our might." That almost summed up his approach to the relationship between the Sangh and the government all along.

Being an ardent nationalist and patriot first and foremost, he acted as a beacon light to guide the nation at every critical twist and turn in its destiny. Unmindful of personal glory, he did not care if he largely went unacknowledged by the country, or its political establishment to be precise. In the mid-fifties when India's political leadership was lulled into inertia by the slogan "Hindi Chini Bhai Bhai," Sri Golwalkar's was the lone voice of caution not to be deceived by the hollow slogan but to fortify our borders. Subsequent events proved how correct he was. Similarly when the Sikh agitation for Punjabi Suba had assumed alarming proportions, he was the first to advise that Punjabi language with Gurumukhi script should be owned by all people in Punjab as their mother tongue. At the heart of all his exhortations was the central 'mantra' of strengthening the unity and integrity of India.

He was deeply distressed by the atrocities committed by Pakistani armed forces in erstwhile East Pakistan before the birth of Bangladesh. He observed : "Its latest action in East Bengal, the unparalleled genocide and uprooting of ten million citizens, has condemned it in the eyes of the world as the most heinous criminal against humanity." And when the Indo-Pak war broke out in 1971, he told the people: -

"Let us now turn to the responsibilities devolving on us, the common people, in times of war. We should concentrate our thoughts and feelings on how best to mobilize and channelize all our energies in a practical way to help our government and enthuse our jawans." (M.S. Golwalkar: "Bunch of thoughts," Third Edition, 1996, published by Sahitya Sindhu Prakashana, Bangalore).

He thus stood up as the unfailing guide of the people at every critical cross-road, kind of an unacknowledged conscience-keeper of the nation. And yet he steered clear of politics and maintained the apolitical character of the Sangh all through. As a 'Sanyasi,' he shunned personal publicity and like Swami Vivekanand, he kept aloof from politics. Whatever he said or observed in the context of the prevailing situation was in his capacity as a true patriot and concerned citizen and not a political leader.

He worked tirelessly till the last day of his life inspite of being seized by a terminal illness. Like Swami Ram Krishna Paramhans, Sri Golwalkar was afflicted with cancer which was steadily taking its toll on his body. And like the Swami himself, he passed away quietly after evening prayers at the Sangh headquarters in Nagpur on 5 June 1973 at the age of 67. He was much maligned by an odd assortment of leftists and miscalled 'secularists' for his vision of Indian nationalism based on the time-honoured Hindu civilization. For those of his critics who have an open mind, here is what he said on the much highlighted and politically abused issue of religious minorities in India: "So, all that is expected of our Muslim and Christian co-citizens is the shedding of the notions of their being 'religious minorities' as also their foreign mental complexions and merging themselves in the common national stream of this soil. As far as the national tradition of this land is concerned, it never considers that with a change in the method of worship, an individual ceases to be the son of the soil and should be treated as an alien.

"Ingrained in this soil is *love and respect for all faiths and religious beliefs. He cannot be a son of this soil at all who is intolerant of other faiths.*" What more could be asked for to prove his so-called 'secular' credentials in the context of his impeccable commitment to vibrant Indian nationalism?

What Sri Golwalkar said above on this issue is quite in keeping with, and in fact follows from, the observations of Swami Vivekananda and Yogi Sri Aurobindo on the all inclusive character of the universalist Hindu civilization. He thus belonged to the same genre of patriotic saints or saintly patriots as the Swami and the Yogi who lit the flame of Indian national resurgence at the beginning of the 20th century. No wonder that even as he was almost demonized by unholy brokers of miscalled 'secularism' in his lifetime, he came to be lionized by acknowledged leaders of Indian society ofter his death.

Smt. Indira Gandhi, then the Prime Minister and a bitter critic of the Sangh, said: "He held a respected position in national life by the force of his personality and the intensity of his conviction, even though many of us could not agree with him". Acharya Binoba Bhave complemented him as a leader with 'a broad national outlook' who had great regard for other religious faiths. The Acharya observed: "He did not have a narrow view of any religion. In fact, he had love for Muslims and only wanted them to join the national mainstream". Jaya Prakash Narain aptly described him as a 'saint'. And both houses of parliament paid tributes to him, even though he was never a member of either house.

The most eloquent tribute was paid to him by the national daily, 'The Indian Express' dated 7 June 1973 in its editorial column. It said: "He had qualities of ancient India's Rishis and Munis. He achieved unparalleled success in cultivating, among the youth, reverence for motherland, dedication to her cause, and discipline and making them work to remove the sufferings of the poor. Next only to Mahatma Gandhi in attracting and influencing the youth, he was also called as the second Vivekananda.. It is rare to see another leader like him."

As a true Karma Yogi in the best traditions of the ancient Hindu civilization, Sri Golwalkar (Sri Guruji) made invaluable contribution to nation building in troubled times and left his indelible imprint on the recent history of India.

24

The Oldest Living Civilisation of the World

Contemporaneous with or perhaps older than the oldest known civilisation of the world, the Hindu civilization is one of the miracles of human history. Based on the Vedas and Vedic traditions, it has continued over thousands of years to define the religiousity of vast majority of people of India described as Hindus. At all life cycle events like birth, marriage, death etc, Vedic hymns are recited and vedic rites performed down to this day. It may be recalled that at the funeral of a self proclaimed agnostic like Jawaharlal Nehru, attended by world leaders, Vedic hymns were recited and ceremonies going back to thousands of years were gone through. The scene was re-enacted at the funeral of his illustrious daughter, Indira Gandhi, the standard bearer of "Secularism" in the country's politics.

S.N. Dasgupta writes :"The laws which regulate the social, legal, domestic and religious customs and rites of the Hindus, even to the present day, are said to be systemized memories of old Vedic teachings and are held obligatory on their authority". (Quoted, in *'A Short History* of *Hinduism'* by Klaus K.

Klostermaier, First South Asian Edition, 2006). This kind of continuity of thousands of years old traditions in the lives of the people is a unique feature of Hindu civilization which is not shared by any other ancient civilization of the world. A. L. Basham observes: *"The ancient civilization of India differs from those of Egypt, Mesopotamia and Greece in that its traditions have been preserved without a break down to the present da...Until the advent of the archaeologist, the peasant of Egypt or Iraq had no knowledge of the culture of his fore fathers..* In each case there had been an almost complete break with the past". (*'The Wonder that was India'*, A.L.Basham, Rupa paper back, 1989).

Mesopotamia, comprising modern Iraq, with parts of eastern Syria and Southern Turkey, was once the seat of a great civilization with its developed technologies of flood control, water storage, drainage, astronomy and mathematics. The most significant component of Mesopotamian civilization was its polytheistic religion involving worship of Air God, Sun God and Moon God, much like the Vedic Gods of Ancient India, with its impressive temples of worship. But there is no trace of the great Mesopotamian civilization in the lives and thoughts of present day Iraqi people. This ancient civilization was totally wiped-out by Arab Islamists when they conquered the Middle East around the middle of the 7th century AD.

The same is true of the ancient Persian civilization which had in its heyday posted a serious challenge to the mighty Greeco-Roman or Hellenic Civilization. Once the Arab Islamists overpowered the Persian Sassanids with their trade mark Zoroastrian religion in 637 AD, not only the native ruling dynasty and Zoroastrian religion but the ancient Persian Civilization itself came to an end.

While Islamism as a politico-religious force wiped out the Mesopotamian and Persian civilizations in the Middle East,

Christianity - the other great proselytizing religion, finished off the long-lasting Hellenic or Greeco-Roman Civilization in Europe. There is one great difference between the two, however. Starting with the 18th century European Renaissance, Christian Europe harked back to the glory of the pagan (nature worshipping) civilization of the Greeco-Romans, their distant ancestors, in matters secular like art and culture with pride. In sharp contrast, Islamism washed all lands that came under its sway clean of their pre-Islamic past.

The Muslim peoples of Iraq and Iran, far from taking pride in their glorious Mesopotamian and Persian heritage, would not even like to remember it today. The great Mesopotamian and Persian civilizations of their past were just wiped off their memory by the rampaging surge of Islamism. The once flourishing Nile Valley civilization of Egypt met the same fate at the hand of the Islamists. It is remembered to day only by the magnificent pyramids built around four and a half thousand years ago. In any case, both Islam and Christianity have the dubious distinction of polishing off the ancient civilizatiors and indigenous religions of the lands and peoples coming under their sway. With such awesome antecedents known to history, Islamists came to rule over India for well over five hundred years and Christian British for over two hundred years. The Islamist rulers bid to erase all traces of Hinduism (Idol breaking, temple destruction, forcible conversions, Jijya tax etc.) is recorded in history.

The British rulers did not resort to those kinds of measures to impose Christianity, but they gave free hand to Christian missionaries to do the job in their own sophisticated way. It was a world-wide phenomenon. Wherever the British or other European powers went in Asia and Africa, the Christian missionaries followed and carried on with the task of converting the local population to Christianity. Referring to Christian missionaries, a black African leader once remarked *"When they came, they had the bible and we had the land; now we have the bible and they have the land."*

In such a historical scenario, it is nothing short of a miracle that the ancient Hindu Civilization survived and remained largely intact inspite of colossal civilizational assault by Islamists and British for well over seven hundred years. It is indeed a wonder of history. How come? What is the basic factor behind this extraordinary survival power of Hinduism or Hindu Civilization?

But, first, what is the time span or age of the Hindu civilization? How old is it? This has been dealt with partially in chapter 4 earlier. The Hindus consider their religious tradition as *'anadi'* that is, beginning -less, and call their religion *'Sanatan Dharma'*, that is the eternal law of righteousness. That, of course, is a matter of faith which need not be subjected to any argumentation. But there can be no dispute about the fact that the Vedas are the authentic fountain-spring of Hinduism and are regarded as such by Hindus today. The issue of determining the age of Hinduism therefore boils down to dating the Vedas or the Vedic period. That would imply fixing the date of the hymns of Rig Veda which is indisputably the oldest of the Vedas. Referring to the hymns of Rig Veda, Klaus K Klostermaier writes: "Despite their great antiquity they are still accepted as the basic scripture of the Sanatan Dharma and thus are probably the oldest religious text still used by a living religion." (*'A Short History of Hinduism'* by Klaus K. Klostermaier, First South Asian Edition 2006).

Taking their cue from 19th century European Indologists like the French Abbe Dubois and German Max Muller, conventional historians date the Rigveda to between 1200 and 1500 B.C. (Before Christ), that is, around 3500 years back. Such a periodisation of Rigveda, the oldest Hindu scripture, is based on the theory of invasion of India by Aryan tribes from North-West propounded by western historians and blindly accepted by others. Accordingly, Regveda was supposed to be the work of the invading Aryan Tribes incorporating the story of their conquest of forts and citadels of the indigenous people of Indus valley and Gangetic plains. But subsequent research and study by some Indian and Western scholars have exposed the hollowness of the Aryan invasion theory itself and rejected it outright as arbitrary and speculative.

In fact, some western scholars like Moriz Winternitz and Indian luminaries like Sri Aurobindo and Bal Gangadhar Tilak had long back rejected the story of invasion of India by Aryans from outside as figment of imagination of some western Indologists. A host of contemporary, scholars, both Indian and Western, like Subhash Kak, N.S. Rajaram, G. Feurstein, D. Frawley and others have stoutly debunked the Aryan invasion theory on solid archeological, geological, astronomical and scientific grounds.

Even a cursory view of the literature of ancient India would make the Aryan invasion theory unacceptable. For instance, there is no mention of any invasion or migration from outside India in the ancient Indian literature like the Vedas, Puranas, Epics, Tamil works and Buddhist or Jain writings. In absence of any literary evidence, the western historians hit upon the supposed affinity between Sanskrit and European languages to conclude that the Sanskrit speaking Vedic Indians were of Indo-European origin having arrived in India from outside. But inter-connectivity among diverse language groups is a different subject of study in itself and cannot be used to prove or disprove any historical proposition.

Impressed by the grandeur of the Vedas, Max Muller and Co assumed that the people who composed the Vedas belonged to the superior Indo-European stock who entered India from the north west as conquering heroes. When the remains of Harappa in Punjab and Mohanjodaro in Sindh were discovered as a result of archaeological excavations in the first half of the 20th century, the European historians promptly filled them into their pre-conceived theory of Aryan invasion. They imagined that Harappa and Mohanjodaro were cities that the invading Aryans led by the Vedic God Indra destroyed and conquered the indigenous dark-skinned people of the Indus valley.

On the basis of this imaginary invasion by Vedic Aryans from outside, they constructed the super structure of a grand Harappan or Indus Valley civilization which according to them preceded the Vedic period and was allegedly destroyed by the invading Aryans.

This imaginary construction of India's pre-history would imply that the Vedic period came later than the Harappan period and that there was a complete break up from the older civilization after the arrival of Vedic Aryans from outside. This is clearly disproved by the fact that there has been remarkable continuity between the archeological artifacts of the Harappan or Indus Valley civilization and subsequent Indian society in respect of arts, crafts, modes of worship and architecture.

Further, according to the conventional historians, the Vedic Aryans were supposed to have invaded and destroyed the Indus settlements along the mighty river Saraswati around 1500 B.C., that is 3500 years ago. But recent satellite photography and geological investigations have established that river Saraswati had dried out completely by 1900 B.C., that is, about 3900 years ago. That would mean around four hundred years before the Aryans were supposed to have invaded the Indus settlements in the Saraswati region. How could it be? The resultant desertification of the dried up Saraswati region and shift of population from there had left no human settlement in the Indus valley. How could the Aryans be supposed to have invaded the Indus settlement in 1500 B.C. when none existed at that point of time ?

On other hand, the Rigveda records the existence of Saraswati river in full glory as a Goddess to whom lavish prayers are addressed. That would mean that Rigvedic hymns were composed well before 1900 B.C. (around 3900 years ago) by when Saraswati river had disappeared or completely dried up. That would mean that Regveda was composed well before 1900 B.C. when Saraswati river was still in existence. In fact, Hindu scriptures reveal a shift of population from the Saraswati region (Rigveda) to the Gangetic plains (Brahamanas and Puranas) over centuries which is also corroborated by archeological finds. The dating of Rigveda to around 1500 B.C. by conventional historians is therefore palpably wrong.

Recent researches by some eminent scholars have revealed that the Regvedic period was not only much older but that the Indus (Harappan) civilization itself was a later 'Vedic phenomenon'. For instance, the town planning and architectural designs of Indus buildings were based on advance algebraic geometry of the kind derived from the Vedic "Sulvasutras". Further, recent excavations have discovered a site larger than Mohanjodaro in Dwarka associated with Lord Krishna. The Mahabharat period in which Lord Krishna figures came at the end of the Vedic period.

Based on similar archaeological and objective evidences, contemporary Indian and western scholars like N.S. Rajaraman and Klausk Klostermaier have fixed the date of composition of Rigveda at 4000 B.C. that is, 6000 years ago, ('Hinduism' : A Short History' by Klausk Klostermier , First South Asian Edition, 2006) . This early dating of Rig Veda , which marks the beginning of Hinduism, pushes back the origin of Hindu civilization by thousands of years.

Accordingly, present day scholars like George Feurstein, Subhash Kak andDavid Frawley have considerable justification in pronouncing that India was the 'cradle of civilization'; that would mean that the grand old Vedic or Hindu civilization was older than the known ancient civilizations like the Mesopotamian, Egyptian, Greek, Persian etc.

This new periodisation of the Vedas makes the survival of Hindu civilization through 6000 years of vicissitudes of history all the more remarkable. More so because history has been a graveyard of civilizations which in their heyday had dazzled the world but have passed into oblivion. *In the midst of the death parade of other ancient civilizations through centuries and millennia, the 'cradle' Hindu civilization has emerged* as *the lone survivor. That perhaps is justification enough for the Hindus to describe their religious tradition as' Sanatan Dharma'.*

It would be relevant at this point to being up the question raised earlier. What is the ambrosia or elixir that accounts for this extraordinary longevity of the time-honoured Hindu civilization?

Apart from the great saviours who appeared from 'age to age' to sustain it, the answer to this pertinent question essentially lies in the basics of Hinduism, dealt with at some length in the Capters that follow.

Part II : The Beauty that is Hinduism

25

Vedanta and Idol-Worship

The longevity of the Hindu Civilization is basically rooted in the core character or essence of Hinduism itself. As already discussed earlier in Chapters 1 and 3, the Vedic religious tradition that goes by the name of Hinduism is aptly described as *Sanatan Dharma* the eternal religion. For it is not a religious creed or cult in the narrow sense of the term or a set of rigid dogmas emanating from a single book or a sole prophet, but an eternal tradition of man's Godward endeavor.

Swami Vivekananda has summed up the essence of Hinduism: "Thus to realize God, the Brahman,........is the aim and end of the whole teaching of the Vedas; and every other teaching, therein contained, represents a stage in the course of our progress thereto.... ... ... work hundreds of lives out, search every corner of your mind for ages and still you will not find one noble religious idea that is not already imbedded in that infinite mine of spirituality." *In Defence of* ***Hinduism***, by Swami Vivekananda, Advaita Ashram, Calcutta, 12th Impression, 1999).

It is this universalist, all inclusive, unifying and ever regenerating character of Hinduism which has enabled it to survive through the ages. Not being bounded by a single Book or a sole Prophet, it easily absorbed all that came from outside and assimilated it as part of its own. The rigid separatism of Islam and its deep hostility to idol worship did pose a big problem but the all-pervasive Hindu civilization took it in its stride and survived through the massive onslaught of Islamism on account of its innate spiritual strength.

Paradoxically, idol worship which has been the most visible target of attack by Islamists all through, has been perhaps the most potent sustainer of Hinduism right up to this day. While intellectual Hinduism was sustained by the spiritual heights of Vedanta, that is faith in the immortal soul or 'Brahman', the common mass of the Hindus have stuck to the 'Sanatan Dharma' because of unshakable faith in their deities whose idols they worship from day to day. All practicing Hindus, rich and poor, the elite and commoner, highly qualified professionals and rustic peasants, have such deep faith in the idols of their deities that they would not give it up for anything. They revel in suffering any amount of physical discomfort and are prepared even to risk their lives just to have a 'darshan' of the idols of their cherished Gods.

This deep religious commitment to their icons or idols is evident in an internationally acknowledged mathematics wizard like Shakuntala Devi keeping an idol of Lord Ganesha with her and a Sunita Williams carrying the idol of Ganesha during her record-breaking space travel. It is the same unflinching faith in their idols that drives thousands upon thousands of the classes as well as the masses to travel for miles on foot against heavy odds for worship at the shrintes of Amarnath and Vaishno Devi in the North, Guruvayoor and Ayappa in the South and Vaidyanath Dham in the East. The devotional fervour of the crowds traveling to these shrines is to be seen to be believed.

The magnet that draws vast multitudes of worshippers to these and similar other shrines is the magnificent mythology associated with each one of them. In fact, mythology is an integral part of every living religion, but it is much more so in case of Hinduism. Being the oldest living religion in the world, Hinduism abounds in beautiful mythologies related to all such famed places of worship which elicit intense devotion of Hindu masses. There are mythologies associated with all major deities of Hindu panthean which are compiled in the 'Puranas' (literally, 'old books') relating to them. There are 18 'Maha Puranas' ('Great Puranas') devoted to the Hindu triumverate of Gods, Brahma, Vishnu and Mahesh, and a large number of 'Upa Puranas' ('Lesser Puranas') related to others. Besides, there are numerous' Sthala Puranas" giving the history of different holy places and describing some miraculous events associated with them. By way of illustration, it would be interesting to describe the mythology associated with the idol of Narain (Vishnu) in the shrine at Guruvayoor as contained in the Guruvaupura purana. This 'Sthal Purana' itself forms part of 'Nardiya Purana' which is one of the 'Maha Puranas' of Vaishnava tradition. According to it, the idol at Guruvayoor is of Narain (Vishnu) who Himself passed it on to Brahma, the God of creation, at the beginning of Padmakalpa. It was through the blessings of this icon of Vishnu that Brahma was able to successfully carry on with his duty of Creation. In course of time, after thousands of Years, Vasudeva and Devaki received this idol and through its grace Lord Krishna was born as their son. After destruction of Kansa, the evil ruler of Mathura, by Lord Krishna, Vasudeva and Devaki moved to Dwaraka and carried the idol with them.

The idol remained with Lord Krishna himself at Dwaraka after the passing away of Vasudeva and Devaki. When time came for Lord Krishna to leave this earth and ascend to Vaikuntha. He directed Uddhava to tell Guru (Brihaspati, the preceptor of Gods) to carry the idol to another holy place because

Dwaraka was going to be heavily flooded. Accordingly, Uddhava approached Guru who came over to Dwaraka accompanied by his disciple Vayu , the Air God, and found the city submerged in deluge. The idol was found floating in water. At the approach of Guru and Vayu, the God of seas Varuna withdrew the water enabling Guru to pick up the idol and place it on Vayu's shoulders. Thereupon, Guru and Vayu set out in search of a suitable holy place to install the idol in course of which they traversed the length and breadth of the country. Then at the invitation of Parsurama, they arrived at Rudratirtha in Kerala where Lord Shiva had his abode. On seeing them, Lord Shiva came up from water and told Guru and Vayu: "This is the very spot you are looking for......This place has been earmarked for Narain's idol.....Both of you may now perform the consecration rites. From now on, this place will be known as "Guruvayur." Offering his worship to the idol, Lord Shiva then left the place for his new abode on the opposite bank at Mammiyur.

The divine origin of the idol described above was, according to the Guruvayupura Purana, narrated to King Janamejaya by the sage Dattatreya. It so happened that King Janamejaya had incurred the curse of serpents by indulging in sacrifice of serpents and was badly affilieted with a virulent form of skin disease. One day sage Dattatreya came to his court and was very much moved by the King's suffering. To enable the king to overcome the evil effect of the serpent's curse, the sage advised him to go to Guruvayur and worship the idol the Lord lnstalled there. "The idol here", said the sage, "is none else than Naraina". As advised by the sage, king Janamejaya went over to Guruvayur and worshipped before the idol there for four months attending all the 12 poojas from early morning to midnight. At the end of it, the king was completely cured of his virulent skin ailment and returned to his capital in full glory.

The grand mythology narrated above has sustained the faith of the common mass of Hindus in idol worship at Guruvayur through the ages. In modern times, the Dutch Army attacked the temple and plundered some of the valuables in 1740. At the end of the 18th century, the Islamist Tippu Sultan came marauding, but the main idol was kept safe in the temple well.

For the Hindu masses, idol worship has all through been- the hall mark of their faith in the eternal religion or 'Sanatan Dharma'. The more the Islamists attacked idol worship and vandalised temples, the greater the tenacity with which the worshippers stuck to their faith in their deities. There are legends galore about how particular idols of deities were protected by their devotees against the Islamist attack during Muslim rule. The idol of Srinathjee (Lord Krishna) in the famous temple at Nathdwara (Rajasthan) near Udaipur, which draws worshippers from all over the world, is a case in point.

The idol of Sri Nathjee lay buried at Gobardhan hill in Brajamandal—the playfield of Lord Krishna. Legend has it that Sri Ballabhacharya - a great Krishna devotee - had a dream directing him to recover the idol and install it at a suitable place for the people to worship. Accordingly, the Acharya dug up the idol and installed it in a grand temple built at the Govardhan hill in 1576. His disciple Soor Das, the greatest Bhakti poet of Hindi literature, was a dedicated worshipper of Sri Nathjee (Lord Krishna) and his poetic work was a product of his deep devotion to the Lord. After the passing away of Ballabhacharya and Soor Das, the idol of Gobardhan hill came under the threat of Islamic idol-breakers. To avoid the threat, the Acharya's followers carried the idol of Sri Nathjee away from Brajamandal to the safe zone beyond Aravali hills in Rajasthan. The idol was re-installed in the famous Sri Nath Temple built at a place now known as Nathdwara about 25 kms. from Udaipur.

The reverence with which the Nathdwara temple is regarded today is a telling example of threat perception reinforcing the Hindus' faith in idol worship. The faith in the Godliness of the idol here was greatly strengthened by the legend associated with its origin and the subsequent threat to it. The fact that the idol had to be taken away from Gobardhan hill in Brajamandal and installed at its present location in Rajasthan to protect it from destruction at the hand of Islamists has only made it more venerable.

This is true of the most holy places of worship for Hindus in India, Mathura and Varanasi. Both the holy cities were repeatedly attacked by Islamists, temples were destroyed and idols broken. Mathura, for instance, was first raided by Mahmud of Ghazni in the year 1017 and his own chronicler records that the sultan's army set fire to temples and broke up a golden image. It was next targeted by the fanatic Mughal ruler Aurangzeb who ordered the destruction of the magnificent Krishna temple in the year 1669. Here again, his record-keeper records in 'Ma-Asiri Alamgiri' that after demolishing the temples, "the richly jeweled idols taken from the pagan temples were transferred to Agra and there placed beneath the steps leading to the Nawab Begam Sahib's mosque.......".

The temple town of Varanasi met similar fate at the hand of Islamic adventurers from time to time. In the year 1194 the Muslim general Qutbuddin Aibak ransacked Varanasi and destroyed nearly a thousand temples. As new temples were built in the succeeding centuries, Sikander Lodi raided and destroyed them in the year 1496. Under the enlightened rule of Akbar, two large temples with idols of Shiva and Vishnu were built a century later, but these were also got demolished during Aurangzeb's rule under his orders. And yet Varanasi continued to be the epicenter of Hindu worship. It may be noted that it was at Varanasi that Goswami Tulsi Das, the illustrious Bhakti poet and author of *Ram Charitra Manas*—lived and worked before the accession of Aurangzeb to power. And after the destruction of temples by Aurangzeb, a Maharashtrian Brahmin named Narain Bhatta organised the reconstruction of Vishwanath Temple at Varanasi. Today, Kashi Vishwanath is one of most revered deities worshipped by Hindus from all over the world.

The tale of the two cities—Mathura and Varanasi - amply illustrates that far from detracting or dampening the Hindu's faith in idol worship, the temple destruction spree of Islamists like Sikandar Lodi and Aurangzeb further reinforced it. In fact, the islamists' rampage against Hindu temples and idol worshippers lent an aura of martyrdom to them. It only strengthened the Hindu's resolve and determination to carry on with idol worship regardless. In one sense, martyrdom is an important element in the religious faith of the people. It was only after crucification that Christ was deified into a God worshipped by Christians all over the world. And martyrdom of prophet Mohammad's grandsons Hasan and Hussein in the battlefield at Karbala elevated them to the status of prophethood in the eyes of Shia Muslims. The martyrdom of Sikh Gurus at the hand of Islamists is a very important factor in Sikh faith.

Amidst the diversity of Hindus' ways of worship, a common thread that runs through all is the performance of 'Pooja' before their deities. Practising Hindus express their devotion to God by performing 'Pooja' in a temple occasionally and at home routinely. And 'pooja' cannot be conceived of without an icon or deity before whom it is performed. In this mode, a God is worshipped in the form of an idol, be it of Rama, Krishna, Shiva or Durga, which is believed to be the repository of divinity. It is both a prayer for wordly benefits and self surrender before the deity. 'Pooja' has come to be the staple of Hindu religiousity and idol worship a trade mark of Hinduism.

As stated earlier, idol-worship has been the most important factor in survival of Hinduism, for the simple reason that it is the easiest way to conceive of God. The heights of Vedanta may be too stiff to scale or comprehend for the simple village peasant and uninitiated urban professional and wage-earner. But the image of his diety comes in easy for him to visualize and relate to. And worship of the image is a way to guide him, even for a while away from his sensual existence towards the God Supreme. Adi Shankaracharya, the high priest of Vedantic concept of oneness of '*Atman*' and '*Brahman*' or Supreme Soul, has also approved of image-worship as a valid first step in man's Godward advance. According to him, "the personal God *(Ishwara)* gradually brings the individual man to realize that the individual self and Ishwara and the limitless Brahman are in .essence the same thing.' ('*The Mind of Adi Shankaracharya*' by Y. Keshava Menon, Jaico, Mumbai, 2005). That goes to show that there is no real dichotomy or contradiction between image-worship and the Vedantic concept of Supreme Soul or 'Brahman'.

Swami Vivekananda said the same thing in more clear terms. He observed: "As to the so-called Hindu idolatory - first go and learn the forms they are going through, and where it is that the worshippers are really worshipping, whether in the temple, in the image, or in the temple of their own bodies. First know for certain what they are doing...And then it will explain itself in the light of the Vedantic philosophy". ('*In Defence of Hinduism*' by Swami Vivekananda, Advaita Ashrama, Calcutta, 12th Impression, 1999).

Although, popular Hinduism is primarily or commonly identified by image-worship, the Hindu faith is not confined to it alone. Hinduism as a whole is too vast a religious stream to be prisoner of any particular mode of worship. Apart from the ancient Vedic rituals and philosophic Vedanta, worship of "*Nirakar*" or "*Nirgun*" (formless) God is as much a part of Hindu tradition as idol worship. Two of the notable Bhakti poets who kept the torch of Hinduism burning during the dark period of

Islamic assault—Kabir Das and Raidas-were worshipper of "Nirgun" or formless God. Both of them were devout worshippers of Rama, but their Rama was not embodied in any idol or image. Their Rama was the 'Nirakar' or formless God Supreme of whom every individual soul was a part or fragment.

And yet, in terms of popular appeal, Kabir Das and Raidas could not match Tulsi Das who worshipped '*Sagun*' God in the form of Rama. For it was far easier for the common mass of Hindus to visualise 'Sagun' Rama in human form and worship his idol. It is through idol worship that an ordinary Hindu peasant or worker has access to the God Supreme who is infinite, unconditioned and cannot be described or defined.

It was given to Swami Rama Krishna Paramhans to beautifully harmonise and co-relate the devotion to impersonal God Supreme ('Brahman' of Vedanta) and personal God of the idol-worshipper. Himself a devout worshipper of Goddess Kali's image since his young days, he identified Her with the Divine Mother who was as much formless as in the form of a deity. To him, the Divine Mother was the Supreme Being, God the Absolute, who transcended all thought, all time and space. He observed: "The key to the realization of the Absolute is with the Divine Person alone, the 'Saguna Brahman' of the upanishads, the personal God of devotees." He went on to elaborate: "So long as you are a person, an individual of your own, God will....... manifest himself to you as a person. Nor can you conceive of, think or perceive God otherwise than as a person, so long as you are a person... ... ...For with the majority of mankind, the ego is a thing which cannot be shaken off in this life.... Thus they (ordinary men) must........meditate upon and commune with the Personal God. For sages and scriptures and revelation all agree in assuring us that the unconditioned does manifest itself to man... ... ... as a conditioned being - the Impersonal as personal God. These Personal Manifestations are by no means less real.." ("The *Condensed Gospel of Sri Rama Krishna',* Sri Rama Krishna Math, Madras, 1978).

Swami Rama Krishna not only synthesized the realization of 'Brahman' (Supreme Soul) of Vedanta and idol worship, but also affirmed the oneness of different manifestations of God worshipped by Hindus. To him, Shiva, Shakti and Vishnu were one and the same - diverse forms in which 'Brahman' or God Supreme manifests Himself. He thereby underlined the basic unity of worshippers of Shiva, Shakti and Vishnu representing varied shades of Hindu worship.

He did not stop at that. Swami Rama Krishna's eclectical approach to religion encompassed in its sweep Islam and Christianity also, bringing about a beautiful symphony of religious faiths. He kept the pictures of not only Hindu Gods and Goddesses including Buddha in his chamber, but also of Jesus Christ. He summed up his view or religious faith in his famous dictum - "It is the same God toward whom all are directing their steps, though along different paths." That is the core value of Hindu civilization which is like a vast ocean accommodating and absorbing any number of streams flowing into it.

26

Sanctuary of Diverse Faiths

That brings up the unique and most distinguishing feature of Hindu Civilisation-understanding and assimilation, and not destruction, of diverse faiths. This was most eloquently stated by Swami Vivekananda in his famous Address to the Parliament of Religions at Chicago, U.S.A., on 11 September 1893. Presenting Hinduism as the mother of religions, he spoke of the over all spirit of tolerance inherent in Hinduism which regards all religions as true. Addressing the final session of the parliament of Religious on 27 September 1893, the Swami observed: "The Christian is not to become a Hindu or a Buddhist, nor a Hindu or a Buddhist to become a Christian. But each must assimilate the spirit of the others and yet preserve his individuality and grow according to his own law of growth." And he gave the logo to be written on the banner of every religion: "Assimilation and not destruction", "Harmony and peace and not dissension" .

Toleration and Accommodation of diverse religious faiths have been the hallmark of Hinduism all through the ages. And it has shown in course of the chequered and yet glorious history of the grand old Hindu Civilization. Right from the ancient times down to the present day, India, the home ground of Hindu civilization, has been a sanctuary of followers of diverse faiths trooping into it for one reason or the other.

Israelis or the Jews

Among the earliest religious communities moving into India and finding safe haven in the land of the Hindus were the Israelis or Jews - the descendents of Abraham, the grand patriarch of the Jewish community. According to the Bible (Old Testament), the Israelis settled in the land of Goshen in Egypt were held as captive labourers by Egyptians and put to immense hardships by their brutal taskmasters. Pharaoh, the king of Egypt, was so alarmed at the growing population of the Hebrews (Israelis) that he ordered his people to throw all new born Israeli boys into the Nile river. Being moved by their miserable plight, Jehovah (their God) one day appeared before Moses and said, "I have seen the deep sorrows of my people in Egypt, and have heard their pleas for freedom from their hard task-masters. I have come to deliver them from the Egyptians and to take them out of Egypt into a good land, a large land, a land 'flowing with milk and honey' ... .." (The Old Testament: Exodus 3.7)

Here a word about Moses. There are biblical legends about the birth of Moses out of marriage between a Hebrew father and an Israeli tribe mother, his upbringing in the royal court of Egypt and subsequent escape from Egypt. Leaving the legends aside, Moses was a historical figure who became the leader of the Jews and promulgator of the famous Ten Commandments. He proclaimed the existence of the one and the only God, the God of Israel, who alone was to be worshipped.

In accordance with his God's command, Moses led the Israeli tribes out of the Nile delta in Egypt towards the south reaching the valley of river Jordan after many many years. Thereafter, according to the biblical story, traveling northwards in search of the promised land being guided by their God from time to time, the Israelis reached the plain of Moab. Realising that he was nearing his end, Moses then delivered a farewell speech to his people, and at last climbed Mount Nebo to see 'the land of milk and honey' promised by God before he passed away. Pointing to the vast area within his gaze, the God told Moses, "It is the Promised Land I promised Abraham, Isaac and Jabcob that I will give it to their descendents. Now you have seen it, but you will not enter it."

The Bible (Old Testament) says: "So Moses, the disciple of the Lord, died in the land of Moab as the Lord had said. The Lord buried him in a valley near Beth-Peor in Moab, but no one knows the exact place."(Dueteronomy, 34:5,6). The Bible, however, describes some land marks regarding the location of Moses' burial site such as the plains of Moab, Mount Nebo, Beth-peor and Heshbon. Taking cue from these land marks, it is possible to locate the burial place of Moses which would also indicate the migration of Israelies to that land.

According to Holger Keisten, the biblical name "Beth-Peor' seems to refer to Behat-poor which in course of time became Bandipur situated in Sopore district of Kashmir. And the biblical 'Heshbon' corresponds to the village Hasha or Hasbal, a few kilometers north-east of Bandipur. In the vicinity of these land mark places, there is a site known as 'Muqam-I-Musa', that is, 'place of Moses'. And a river bank in Bijbihara (Kashmir) is known as 'Moses' bath place even today. Further, the rocks at the confluence of the rivers Jhelum and Sind (not the Indus) near Shadipur to the north of Srinagar are known as 'Kohna-I-Musa' (cornerstone of Moses). These landmarks bearing the name of Moses as Musa are clear indicators of Presence of Moses and his Jewish tribes in India's Kashmir valley. ('Jesus Lived in India, Holger Keisten, Penguin Books, India, 2001)

Next to Moses, who is a mythological as well as a historical figure, King Solomon is the most important leader of Isrealis known to the world. It was during the reign of Solomon's father, King David, that the twelve Israeli tribes were united into one national whole. And it was during Solomon's reign that the famous Jewish Temple was built at Jerusalem, the capital of unified Israeli or Jewish tribes. Solomon is known world-wise for his words of wisdom.

There are legends about Solomon's presence in Kashmir. It is said that it was Solomon who got a channel created in the mountain range through which water flows into the Dal Lake. And it was he who built a small temple on the hill over looking Srinagar which is still known as 'Takht-I-Suleman', that is, 'throne of Solomon'. The hill is also known as Shankaracharya hill since Adi Shankaracharya ascended it during his visit to the northernmost tip of the country. The coming of Solomon and his Jewish tribes in Kashmir is corroborated by the fact that Kashmir valley is referred to by the locals as 'Bagh-I-Suleman" that is the 'Garden of Solomon'. In local parlance 'Solomon' became 'Suleman' just as 'Moses' had become 'Musa'.

After Solomon's death around 930 B.C., the Israeli kingdom was split into two parts. Out of the original twelve Israeli tribes, the ten tribes of the North formed the state of Israel and the two tribes of the South constituted the state of Judah. Subsequently, the northern state of Israel was conquered by the neighbouring Assyrians of Mesopotamia who deported the ten Israeli tribes out of their land. Most of them moved towards the East and were never heard of in their homeland again. They are still described as 'the ten lost tribes of Israel', as if vanished into the thin air.

"But there are many clear indications", writes Holger Kersten, "that most of these 'lost tribes of Israel', after centuries of homeless wandering...finally arrived at their Promised Land... Northern India, where they have enjoyed peace and tranquility to the present day." That would go to show that the world's most persecuted religious community - the Israelis or Jews - continued to seek and find a safe haven in India, since the earliest of times. The leading Israeli figures known to history - Moses and Solomon - and their 'ten lost tribes' found their sanctuary in this land of the great Hindu civilization.

Christ and St. Thomas

To cap it all, Holger Kersten, the author referred to above, has come out with the astounding story of Jesus Christ Himself coming to India at a young age and learning from the Buddhist teachings and the Veda. An enterprising German scholar specializing in religious history, Holger Kersten traveled to different parts of India during 1970's and made intensive research on Jesus Christ's India connection. His painstaking effort resulted in a book, first published in Germany in 1983, the very title of which gives out the gist of his findings-"Jesus Lived In India." He revised the contents in the light of comments of "discerning critics" and came out with a fresh edition of the book in 1993 affirming his claim about Christ's presence in India.

The book begins with a reference to a similar research carried out by a Russian scholar - Nicolai Notovitch - about a hundred years before. Towards the end of 1887, Notovitch traveled to northern India and eventually reached a Buddhist monastery in Ladakh. In course of conversation with the Lama there, he learnt that the monastery was in possession of written accounts about the mysterious prophet Issa, which strikingly resembled the legends abut Jesus Christ. On his earnest request, the Lama subsequently read out the story of Issa from bound sheets of loose leaves stored in the monastery, interpreted by an interpreter- Notovitch meticulously recorded the contents of the document, as interpreted to him, in his travel diary. From the contents of the Lama's document noted in his travel diary, Notovitch produced a book entitled 'The unknown life of Jesus Christ', first published in French in 1894. Holger Kersten outlines the contents of the book broadly as follows.

In far away Israel, a divine infant was born and given the name Issa (Arabic name for Jesus). In the 14th year of his life, the young Jesus arrived in the Indus region (India) in the company of merchants, "and he settled among the Aryans, in the land beloved of God, with the intention of perfecting himself and of learning laws of the great Buddha." Then he traveled through the land of five rivers (the Punjab) and arrived at Jagannath where the "Priests of Brahma" welcomed him. Here Jesus learned to read and understand the Veda. After spending six years in Jagannath, Rajgriha, Benares and other holy cities, he reached Nepal in the Himalayan ranges. He stayed in Nepal for another six years dedicating himself to the study of Buddhist scriptures. Finally he moved towards the west and reached his homeland Palestine to redeem his people and restore true faith among them.

That was the story contained in the Russian scholar's book published in 1894 and narrated by Holger Kersten in his recent book referred to above. During 1970's - 80's, Holger Kersten himself traveled to India and carried out an in-depth research into Christ's India connection. And he came broadly to the same conclusions as Notovitch had done around a hundred years earlier about Christ' visit to and stay in India in his young days. He cites striking similarities between the teachings of Buddha and Christ as supportive evidence of Christ's stay in India prior to his preachings in his home land, Palestine, and eventual crucification.

For instance, just as Buddha rejects blood sacrifice by some orthodox priests, Jesus criticizes blood sacrifice by Jews. Buddha denounces the orthodox practices of the priestly castes of Brahmans which had been reduced to meaningless rituals and burdensome regulations. Similarly, Jesus criticizes the orthodox Jews for laying heavy burdens on men's shoulders, 'but they themselves will not move them with one of their fingers. The Hindu 'Sanyasis' and Buddhist monks were told to renounce everything in their spiritual pursuit. In the same way, Christ asked his disciples to go out and proclaim his message renouncing all material things like gold, silver and even extra clothing. Buddha spoke in parables and so did Christ. Like Buddha said when blind people hold on to each other in a line, they see nothing, and Christ said that a blind man cannot lead another blind man without both falling into a ditch. Some of the parables told by Christ reflect the ancient Hindu traditions like the famous saying that faith can move mountains. This would seem to be derived from the episode of Lord Krishna relocating the mountain Gobardhana to protect the inhabitants from the wrath of the rain God Indra.

There are any number of legends about Buddha and Christ which are remarkably similar. Buddha crosses the river Ganges in flood and Christ walks across the water of the lake. Once when Buddha was standing on the bank of a river, a disciple standing on the opposite bank started walking across on the water towards him. Similarly Peter once approached Christ by walking on top of water. Buddha's disciple started sinking in the river when he lost meditation on Buddha and was saved only when he regained his contemplation of the Master. In a similar manner, Peter started sinking in the water when his faith began to waver, but was saved by the grace and soothing words of Christ. "Walking on water", writes Holger Kersten, "is a concept quite unheard of in Jewish traditions, but is a theme that is wide spread in India: it is more than possible that the New Testament adopted the idea from there." And he goes on to add that "more than one hundred passages in the New Testament may be cited that exhibit evidence of sources that hark back to a much older tradition : Buddhism."

And more Holger Kersten has come out with the startling proposition that Jesus Christ not only stayed in India during his formative youthful years, but he survived the crucification and returned back to live in India. He spent the rest of his life in India as an itinerant teacher until his death at a ripe old age. Based on his critical analysis of biblical texts and extensive research on the ground, Holger Kersten gives out a new Jesus story after crucification. "In Jesus case" he writes, "there were a total of twenty-eight wounds that continued to bleed even after his removal from the cross. This proves that Jesus could not possibly have been dead when his body was laid in the tomb." The rest of the story, as narrated by Kersten in his book, is as follows.

As Jesus hung unconscious from the Cross, Joseph and Nicodemus took him out and brought him to the nearby rock-tomb. In the isolation of the tomb, preparations for healing of his wounds began, even as the opium drink helped him to sleep deeply, relieved of pain. As soon as he was physically able to move, he was quickly shifted away from the reach of the hostile Jewish authorities. So when the women (Mary Magdalene and Salome) came to the tomb with oils for anointing what was supposed to be Christ's dead body at the end of Sabbath on Monday morning, the body was just not there. They found the heavy stone rolled aside, the entrance open and the tomb empty.

Thus, according to Kersten, Jesus recovered from the wounds inficted during crucification and proceeded to Damascus in the middle of Syria, about 300 kilometers to the north of Jerusalem. He was reasonably safe here from his persecutors because Jews were hated at Damascus. It was also the centre of Essene religious community whose protection he could avail of. There is a place about five kilometers outside Damascus which is still known as 'Mayyam-I-Isa' (The Place where Christ lived).

Then onwards, Jesus kept on traveling eastwards through Parthia (modern Iraq and Iran) with stop-overs at different stations along the old Silk Route. And eventually, he reached India (Kashmir), his final resting place where he lived until his passing away after a long eventful life. During the time Christ lived in Kashmir, it was ruled by the Great King Kanishka -I of the Kushan dynasty, a Buddhist himself who followed a policy of religious toleration.

In the Foreword to his path breaking book, Holger Kersten writes: "Some of the assertions I make may seem audacious, some even improbable, but I have tried to provide solid evidence for all the claims I have put forward, and to support them with reference to genuinely trustworthy sources". Referring to the understandable rejection of the story of Christ in India by traditional Christian circles, be observes: "It is hard indeed to kick against the current of almost two thousand years of deeply rooted convention. All the same, just because a story has been told for two thousand years does not mean that it is true." ("Jesus Lived In India", by Holger Kersten, Penguin books India, 2001)

The notable aspect of Kersten's story about Christ's presence in India is that it brings out in bold relief the tolerant and accommodative character of Hindu civilization all through the ages. For it was in course of his travels to escape from his sworn persecutors - the Jews and the Romans - that he is claimed to have come and found a safe haven in this land which has always sheltered persecuted communities from all over the world.

While this claim may be disputed by traditional Christian quarters, there can be no dispute about another Great Christian apostle - St. Thomas - coming to India and preaching his gospel here. St. Thomas, it may be noted, was closest to Jesus Christ among his original twelve disciples. According to "Gospel of Thomas" and "Acts of Thomas", St. Thomas had become an altar ego of Jesus addressed even as 'Twin brother of Christ.' He lived and preached in South India winning a good number of adherents in the coastal areas. They are still known as 'Thomas

Christians' or 'Syrian Christians' because St. Thomas had his roots in Edessa, Syria, where he had preached earlier. ' Syrian Christians' are the earliest Christian community in India with a significant presence in the modern South Indian state of Kerala. And the tomb of St. Thomas is still present in the small town of Mylapore, a few kilometers from Madras (now named Chennai).

The Zoroastrians or Parsees

The most glaring case of a severely persecuted religious community finding shelter in Hindu India is that of the Zoroastrians of Persia, now known as Iran. Zoroastrians are the followers of an ancient religion founded in Persia by their prophet Zoroaster (that is Zarathustra) long before the birth of Christianity. Zoroaster, like Moses and Jesus, is both a historical and mythological figure. According to Greek mythological writers, he became the Prophet of a new religion in his 30th year when God appeared before him seated on a throne of fire and bestowed His sacred law upon him. That explains why Zoroastrians are known for their worship of fire.

Zoroastrianism became the official religion when Ardeshir I, an ardent follower of the religion, became the ruler of Persia in the year 226 A.D. His dynasty, known as the Sassanid dynasty, ruled over Persia for over four centuries during which Zoroastrianism reigned supreme in Persia (Iran). But when the Arab Islamists conquered Persia in the year 637 A.D., not only the native Sassanid Empire but the Zoroastrian religion also was wiped out of the country. To escape severe religious persecution at the hand of the Islamists, the followers of Zoroastrian religion fled from Persia. A good number of them came over to India, "which welcomed them as she has welcomed all others who have come to her seeking refuge. The Parsis in India today are the descendents of these Zoroastrians". (Jawaharlal Nehru in his "Glimpses of World History.") The once thriving Zoroastrian religion, banished from its land of birth, survives today in the land of the ancient Hindu civilization which has ever been a sanctuary of diverse faiths seeking shelter in it. This was clearly highlighted by Swami Vivekananda in his famous address to the Parliament of Religions held in Chicago, U.S.A. in September 1893.

The Baha'is or Followers of Bahaullah

And this tradition continues down to this day. In modern times, India has given shelter to the followers of Baha'i faith, badly mauled and persecuted in the Islamic state of Iran which was the land of its origin. The brutal suppression of Baha'i religious community by the Islamic regime in Iran is a widely known fact in the world today. The United Nations, Amnesty International and the European Union have all affirmed that Baha'is have been subjected to arbitrary arrests, wrongful imprisonments, beatings, torture and even unjustified executions in Iran for the only fault of practicing their religion.

The Baha'i faith grew out of Babism, a religious order established in Persia (Iran) in the year 1844 in the teeth of violent opposition by Islamic Mullahs. The Bab himself, the founder of the Babi movement, was imprisoned in 1846 and was eventually executed. In 1863, Bahaullah, a follower of Babism, took up the mantle of the Bab and established what has come to be known as Baha'ism or Baha'i faith.

The Baha'i religion rests on the concept of a single, omniscient, omnipresent God almighty, the creator of all things, who is eternal, without a beginning or end. This is strikingly similar to the Hindu scriptural concept of the God supreme being 'anadi' and 'anant'. And further, according to Baha'i faith, God expresses Himself through a series of divine messengers known as Manifestations of God from time to time. The Manifestations or Messengers, according to Bahaullah, included Abraham, Moses, Zoroaster, Krishna, Buddha, Jesus and Muhammad. This would appear to have come out of traditional

Hindu belief in 'Avatars' or incarnations of God to redeem mankind from time to time.

This was very clearly brought out by Lord Krishna when he showed his form of the universal, infinite and primal God to Arjun as depicted in the 'Mahabharata'. His famous proclamation in Geeta' says :

"यदा यदा ही धर्मस्य ग्लानिर्भवती भारत :....... धर्म संस्थापनार्थाय सम्भवानि युगे युगे।"

"Whenever there is decline of righteousness O Bharata (Arjun) ...then to re-establish righteousness, I create myself from age to age."

The stamp of Hinduism is thus clearly discernible in the Baha'i teachings. And this has been anathema to Islamist regimes in Iran ever since the birth of Baha'ism in that country.

Bahaullah challenged traditional Islamic beliefs, especially the finality of Muhammad's prophethood which is the corner stone of Islam. As a result, the followers of Bahaullah were not only placed outside the domain of Islam but were also regarded as renegades or apostates from Islam who must choose between repentance or death. Accordingly Baha'is were severely persecuted in Iran right through since the beginning of the sect in the 19th century.

The Baha'i persecution continued even during the reign of the Shah of Iran, Mohammad Reza Shah Pahalvi, during mid 20th century. During the month of Ramadan in 1955, a fanatic Islamic preacher, Mohammed Falsafi, indulged in fiery anti-Baha'i rhetoric in his sermons, which caused large-scale mob violence against the Baha'is. As a result, Baha'i properties were destroyed, Baha'i cemeteries descreted, Baha'i people killed, some even hacked to pieces, and Baha'i women abducted and forced to marry Muslims.

Needless to say, the persecution of Baha'is increased manyfold since the advent of Iran's Islamic Revolution in 1979. With the installation of Ayatollah Khomeini as the Supreme leader of Iran, a more systematic and coordinated campaign of persecution started to wipe Baha'ism out completely. So much so that Baha'is are not even recognized as a religious minority like Zoroastrians and Christians in the Islamic Constitution of Iran. In February 1991, a confidential circular issued by the Supreme Cultural Council and signed by the Supreme Leader, Khamenei, himself prescribed the methods of oppression to suffocate the Iranian Baha'is through more 'silent' means. No wonder that the followers of Bahaullah have been virtually squeezed out of Iran where he lived and propounded his faith. As a result, out of a total population of around five and half-million Baha'is across the world, only about three lacs (less than even half a million) continue to live in Iran to suffer worst kind of religious persecution in the land of their origin.

And here again, as in the case of Zoroastrians earlier, the much persecuted Baha'i community has found a safe haven in India, the hallowed land of the Hindu civilization. The Baha'is are not only free to live here and practice their faith in complete security, but also to propagate the teaching of Bahaullah. Since what Bahaullah preached appears to be in essence an outgrowth of Hinduism, many Hindus of elite class have chosen to be his followers without coming out of the Hindu fold. They are happy to be counted as Baha'is, as well as Hindus, because of basic harmony between the two.

It is a measure of full religions freedom enjoyed by Baha'is in India that out of an estimated 5.5 million Baha'is in the world, about 2.2 millions live in India alone. That is, the largest Baha'i community in the world has found shelter in the Hindu land of India, while only around three lacs have been left in Iran, the country where the faith originated. They have built a magnificient Baha'i House of Worship in India's capital which is visited by Baha'is from all over the world. The dome of the Temple is Lotus shaped which has earned it the name of the Lotus Temple. And, significantly enough, lotus is a sacred symbol of Hindus and Jains as well.

The Theosophists

Last but not the least important are the Theosophists who originated in America and have found their permanent home in India. Founded by Colonel H.S. Olcott, an American, and Madame Helena Petrovna Blavatsky, a Russian, the Theosophical movement was formally inaugurated in New York, U.S.A., in November 1875. Beginning with the idea of collecting and diffusing knowledge of the laws which govern the universe, the objectives of the Theosophical Society were formulated as follows :-

"1. To form a nucleus of an Universal Brotherhood of Humanity without distinction of race, creed or colour;

2. To promote the study of Aryan and other Eastern literature, religions, science and vindicate its importance;

3. To investigate the hidden mysteries of nature and the psychical powers latent in man."

While Col. Olcott was the Chief Organiser of the Theosophical Society, Madame Blavatsky was the main ideologue of the Theosophical movement and the spirit behind it. She defined the organization as a society of those dissatisfied with the contemporary materialistic sciences. She observed : "We are the living protest against the crass materialism of our day". (*"The Dawning of the Theosophical Movement"* by Michael Gomes, the Theosophical Publishing House, Wheaton, IL, U.S.A., 1987).

Madame Blavatsky's infatuation with India, which eventually brought her and Col. Olcott to take up residence here, is evident in all her writings. She was enchanted by the thought of an ancient civilization existing in India from the earliest of times dispensing arts, sciences and spiritual thoughts to the rest of the world. It was her vision of India's ancient Hindu Civilisation which induced an irresistible urge in Col. Olcott to come "to the land of the Rishis and Buddhas, the Sacred Land among lands." (Quoted in Michael Gome's book referred to above).

Col. Olcott and Madame Blavatsky were highly impressed by Swami Dayanand Saraswati and his Arya Samaj which was a religious reform movement based on the Vedas as the fountain-spring of Hinduism. At one stage, they were even thinking of merging the Theosophical Society with Arya Samaj with Swami Dayananda as the head. Though the idea of merger did not materialize, their identification with Swami Dayananda's view of the glory that was India's Vedic past was complete. In fact, their cherished desire to see Swami Dayananda in person and hear directly on the Vedic religion was a factor in Col. Olcott and Madame Blavatsky deciding to come to India.

Accordingly, they set upon their, 'Pilgrimage to India' in December 1878, and after spending 17 days in England on their way, Olcott and Blavatsky landed at Bombay early in the morning of 16 February 1879. On arrival in what she called Hindustan, Madame Blavatsky felt "as if the light of the West were bidding us, people from America, good-bye, while the light from the East greeted the new-comers from far-off lands." And on reaching the land, the first thing that, Col. Olcott did was to perform puja. "He stooped down and touched the ground. They were at last on sacred soil". ('The Dawning of the Theosophical Movement' by Michael Gomes, Theosophical Publishing House, Wheaton, IL. U.S.A.)

The Baha'is in the 20th Century and Zoroastrians earlier had been compelled by severe religions persecution at home to seek refuge in India. The Theosophists, on the other hand, were charmed by the spiritual beauty of Hinduism to come to what they called the "sacred" land of India. There was no compulsion or adverse circumstance at home. Theosophy was a growing movement in America. By 1886, twelve American branches in different cities organized themselves into the American Section of the Theosophical Society. The idea of launching the Theosophical movement in England had been mooted by Col. Olcott in November 1877 and the British Theosophical Society was formally founded in June 1878. The movement was evidently spreading in the West. And yet Col. Olcott and Madame Blavatsky chose to come to India and set up their base here because the universalist Hindu Civilisation attracted them like a magnet.

Col. Olcott almost said as much when at a meeting of Theosophists and Swami Dayanand in India in May 1879, he observed: "The God preached by the Swami upon Vedic authority is an Eternal, Boundless, Uncreate, Impersonal Principle satisfying the highest aspirations of spiritual man - a concept ennobling and worthy of reverence." (Quoted 'The Dawning of the Theosophical Movement' by Michael Gomes, referred to earlier.) Having arrived at their spiritual home in India, Olcott and Blavatsky never looked back to their Western roots. Eventually, they set upthe International Headquarters of the Theosophical Society at Adyar near Madras (Chennai) in December 1882, where it is still located today.

Both the founders of the Theosophical Movement lived the rest of their eventful lives at Adyar in India preaching universal brotherhood and search for truth, which forms the basis of all religions, to their fellow theosophists all over the world. After having established the Theosophical Society on a firm footing as a beacon light for seekers of Truth and Divine

Wisdom world-wide, Madame Blavatsky passed away in 1891 and Col. Olcott in 1907. An inscription engraved on the pedestal of their plaster statues at Adyar reads: "The Founders of the Theosophical Society: Helena Petrovna Blavatsky 1831-1891 - Henry Steel Olcott 1832 - 1907."

Among the successors of Col. Olcott as President of the Theosophical Society were such eminent personalities as Dr. Annie Besant and Dr. G.S. Arundale. Annie Besant, it may be noted, was actively associated with the Home Rule movement which formed the background of our freedom movement. And Dr. G.S. Arundale was a prominent figure in India's cultural renaissance of early 20th Century.

While the followers of other faiths who found their sanctuary in India maintained their separate identity, more or less, thanks to the liberal and tolerant ethos of Hindu civilization, the Theosophists merged themselves into Hinduism and became a part of it. In fact, it was the universal world-view of Hinduism based on insights of sages and seers since earliest of times which attracted Col. Alcott and Madame Blavatsky to come to India in the first place and deliver the message of Theosophy in congenial environment. No wonder that the Theosophical Movement grew within the Hindu fold right from its inception in India and has remained so down to this day. As a result Theosophy, inspite of its origin in America, has come to be a part of intellectual Hinduism. And like Aryasamaj is and Kabirpanthis, the Theosophists have come to be indistinguishable part of the great Hindu fraternity.

27

The Indefinable Hindu

The Hindu Civilisation, which is, in essence, a synonym of the Indian Civilisation, is defined by the socio-cultural and religious tradition known as Hinduism. Any discussion about the distinguishing marks of Hindu Civilisation, therefore, boils down to an analysis of the essentials of Hinduism. What exactly is Hinduism has been briefly touched upon earlier. Sri Aurobindo's designation of Hinduism as 'Sanatan Dharma' (eternal religion) at the end of Chapter-3 gives a fair idea of the religious tradition that goes by that name. Perhaps the best definition of Hinduism is that it cannot be defined in terms of the straight-jacket of conventional religion.

The only definitive factor about Hinduism is that it is a religious tradition of Indian origin. The term 'Hindu' was perhaps originally a geographical term used to designate the inhabitants of the region around the river Indus corresponding to the Vedic river 'Sindhu'. The Rig-Veda mentions the land of the Aryans as 'Sapta Sindhu', that is the land of the seven rivers of north-west Indian sub-continent, one of them being 'Sindhu'. The term 'Hindu' is actually derived from 'Sindhu', the original Sanskrit name of what is now known as Indus. The name 'India' is the

Greek and Latin adaptation from the word 'Indus' which is the Persian adaptation from the Sanskrit word 'Sindhu.'

Thus the name 'India' itself, attached to our country as a whole, has been derived from 'Indus' river which is the same as the Vedic river 'Sindhu'. Incidentally, that underlines the basic oneness of Hinduism and Indianism. For, etymologically, both are derived from the name 'Sindhu' or 'Indus', the river. The simplest distinguishing mark or defining attribute of Hinduism, therefore, is the aroma of the soil of our country which sets it apart from other religions originating in foreign lands.

Talking about the 'Indefinable Hindu', M.S. Golwalkar observed: "We existed when there was no necessity for any name. We were the good, the enlightened people, we were the people who knew about the laws of nature and the laws of the spirit. We built a great Civilisation, a great culture and an unique social order. We had brought into actual life almost everything that was beneficial to mankind.. ..So, here we are, Hindus, though defying all definitions, all the same a reality. The Hindu society is a living reality which all of us feel and experience in every drop of our blood. But though we cannot define it, we can and must be able to appreciate the special features which mark out the Hindus as a distinct people." ('Bunch of Thoughts" M.S. Golwalkar, published by Sahitya Sindhu Prakashan, Bangalore, Reprint October 2000.)

Before dwelling upon some of the notable 'special features', it would be relevant to touch upon the basics of Hinduism. Being the Oldest living religion in the world, Hinduism is rooted in the historical Vedic tradition of Iron Age India. Referred to as 'Sanatan Dharma' (eternal religion) by its followers, Hinduism essentially is a vehicle of the basic human urge to discover and connect with the Ultimate Reality, call it by whatever name like the Supreme Soul, Primal Source of all creation or God Supreme. In practical life, it seeks to unveil the principles and practices that would lead any individual to become a better human being living in harmony with 'dharma', that is, righteousness. As such, it is concerned primarily with the human situation rather than an exclusive sectarian situation, which makes its canvas wide and large.

Here is what Mahatma Gandhi, the most illustrious humanist of modern age, had to say about Hinduism. When asked in 1936 what was his religion, the Mahatma replied: "My religion is Hinduism, which for me is the religion of humanity and includes the best of all religions known to me." That said it all about the all embracing, Universalist character of Hinduism which has sustained it through the ages. This is so because unlike other major religions of the world, Hinduism has no single founder or book of revelation. The scriptures of Christianity and Islam, for instance, are supposed to be revealed from a divine source through a single Prophet. The sole prophet of Christianity is Jesus Christ and that of Islam Mohammad. And the single book of divine revealation is the New Testament for Christians and the Qoran for Muslims. Not so in case of Hinduism. There is no single Prophet or book of revealation laying down an established doctrine by which the Hindu people are ordained to abide. The Hindu scriptures, on the other hand, are the accumulated treasures of spiritual truths and laws discovered by our sages and seers over many centuries. They refined and elaborated the spiritual texts which were transmitted orally for a long time before being written down.

28

The Hindu Scriptures

I The 'Shrutis'

The vast body of Hindu scriptures is divided broadly into 'Shruti' (That which is heard or revealed) and 'Smriti' (That which is remembered). These texts dwell upon theology, philosophy and mythology throwing light on the practice of 'dharma', that is righteousness or righteous living.

The 'Shruti' refers to the Veda, which literally means knowledge par excellence or supreme knowledge. What is collectively known as the Veda actually comprises four Vedic texts namely the Rigveda, the oldest one, Yajurveda, Samveda and Atharveda. Taken together, the four Vedas constitute the earliest record of Hindu scriptures.

The Vedas, in their wider meaning, consist of four parts - the 'Samhita', 'Brahmana', 'Aranyaka' and 'Upanishad'. The first and the most identifiable part of the Vedas are 'Samhitas'. These are collections of hymns, prayers, benedictions and sacrificial rituals. The Rigveda (its 'Samhita') has 1028 hymns, which probably were the earliest literary work in the world. The Samaveda consists of 1549 musical hymns used in connection with sacrifice. The Yajurveda contains prose sentences, some of which are poetical and rhythmic, regarding rituals. The Atharveda which contains 73 hymns, is a book of incantations and spells. So much about the 'Samhitas'.

The 'Brahmanas' are prose texts dwelling upon various sacrificial rites and ceremonies. Each 'Samhita' of one or the other of the Vedas has its own "Brahmana' as explanatory texts for the rituals prescribed in it. There are also numerous legends scattered through the 'Brahmanas', which give a comprehensive view of sacrificial ceremonials.. These legends also throw light upon the earliest metaphysical thoughts of the Hindus.

The "Aranyakas" literally mean 'forest treatises' meant for wise old men who had retired into the forests for quiet contemplation. As such the 'Aranyaksas' consist of teachings not related to sacrifies and rituals but dealing with mysticism and philosophy. These are generally considered as the concluding parts or chapters of the 'Brahmana'.

The most important components of the Vedas from the point of view of the religious thoughts of the Hindu family of religions are the Upanishads. These are not only end parts of the Vedas but also their end product and true end or purpose. Also referred to as 'Vedanta' ('End of the Veda'), the Upanishads contain sacred observations designed to teach the means of liberation from re-birth and all suffering, that is, salvation. These are some kind of lectures delivered by dedicated teachers who had dug deep into the secrets of the universe on questions like 'what is the soul, 'what is the universe?' etc. The Upanishads are, thus, more in the nature of wonderful philosophical treatises rather than conventional religious teachings in the narrow sense of the term.

The Upanishads have grown in number in course of time with a number of sectarian and other texts coming up in that name. But the original principal Upanishads are only ten or twelve which have been commented upon by sages like Adi Shankaracharya and other well-known classical commentators. Some of the more important principal Upanishads are Isa, Kena, Katha, Ateraya, Chandogya and Brihadaranayaka. C. Rajagopalachari described the Upanishads as "the most ancient of the world's holy books, still the most modern and most satisfying." Another great scholar of ancient Indian history and religion, K.M. Munshi observed: "Age after age, the best of Indian from the mystical Vaishnava to modern Gandhi found self-fulfilment in living up to an ideal of conduct in accordance with a code of life which may be traced back to the Upanishads." As mentioned earlier, Upanishads are not only the fountain-spring of the highest form of intellectual and philosophical Hinduism but also the basic source of some other religions of the Hindu family like Buddhism and Jainism.

The Vedic scriptures comprise all the four Vedas and their Samhitas, Brahmanas, Aranyakas and Upanishads. That is why the term Veda is often used in the plural to mean the whole range of these sacred texts. The Veda is thus not a single book like the Bible or Qoran but a collection of sacred literature handed down from generation to generation through centuries and millennia. The Veda, in this holistic meaning, constitutes the highest religious authority for Hindus. All their social, legal, domestic and religious customs and rites are based on systematized memories of ancient Vedic teachings.

Many of the hymns of the Rig Veda (Samhitas) are addressed not necessarily to Gods and Goddesses but to the beautiful phenomena of nature like the vast sky, shining Sun, gleaming moon etc, which are glorified in themselves and invoked. Only gradually, the songs of the Rigveda transform these natural phenomena into Gods and Goddesses such as Surya (Sun), Agni (Fire), Maruts (Storms), Usha (Dawn) and Prithvi (Earth). These mythological figures have thus emerged from the personification of some of the most prominent natural phenomena in the songs of the Rigveda.

But Veda, or Rig Veda to be precise, is not all about animistic worship of nature only. As Adi Shankaracharya has pointed out, this kind of worship of prominent elements of nature personified as Gods is meant for the beginners of spiritual pursuits. For higher level of seekers, the Veda in its wider connotation leads to the sublime realization of one God as the Ultimate Reality as conceptualized in the Upanishads which are integral part of the Veda. The evolution from simple animistic worship of nature to the idea of God as the single Ultimate Reality is the most remarkable feature of the Veda.

It may be noted that worship of elements of nature as Gods and Goddesses was also practiced by the Sumerians of Mesopotamia, as mentioned earlier. The Greeko-Romans also had their nature Gods like Zeus and Jupiter corresponding to the Rig Vedic Dyaw (Sky). But these other ancient religions stopped at that. The Vedic religious tradition, on the other hand, developed further and evolved the central idea of 'Param Brahman' or the one Supreme Soul as the source of all creation. That is the real beauty of the Vedic religion, now known as Hinduism.

The Vedas are generally revered by Hindus as books of eternal verities revealed to or discovered by the ancient 'Rishis' (Sages), but nor necessarily of divine origin. They are regarded rather as end-product of spiritual endeavours and search for the Ultimate Truth or God by our ancient sages and seers. That left immense scope for refinement of the texts and diverse commentaries on them by theologians from time to time. In modern, current Hindu belief, the scriptures are not necessarily interpreted literally but in terms of the ethics and metaphorical meanings derived from them. That keeps the scripture alive and updated through commentaries and rational interpretations in the context of changing social conditions.

Here, again, is Mahatma Gandhi's take on this, as recorded in his periodical 'Young India': "The reader will note that I have purposely refrained from using the word 'divine origin' in reference to the Vedas or any other scriptures. My belief in the Hindu scriptures does not require me to accept every word and every verse as divinely inspired. Nor do I claim to have any first-hand knowledge of these wonderful books. But I do claim to know and feel the truth of the essential teaching of the scriptures."

II Smritis

The religious texts other than the 'Shrutis' (the Vedas including the Upanishads) discussed above, are collectively termed as 'Smritis' (those that are remembered). The term is wide and broadly comprises a number of heterogeneous works which owe their authority to the standing of the writer to whom they are attributed. But they are authoritative only to the extent to which they conform to the 'Shrutis' which are the core group of Hindu scriptures. 'Yagyavalkya-Smriti', attributed to an important Vedic seer, and 'Vishnu-Smriti' are some notable 'Smritis' which are regarded as authoritative. But 'Manu-Smriti', attributed to the ancient law-giver Manu, prescribing a code of law based on the occupational caste system is controversial and unacceptable in modern Hindu society.

(a) The 'Puranas' ('old Books')

The more important components of Smritis are the 'Puranas' which dwell upon the creation of the universe, rules of righteous living and, above all, the wonderful mythologies of Hinduism. The mythologies are related to the gods and goddesses they are dealing with. As briefly mentioned in Chapter 25, there are 18 'Maha Puranas' ('Great Puranas') devoted to the major deities of Hindu Pantheon namely, Brahma, Vishnu and Mahesh. Of these, six each are related to the Gods Brahma, Vishnu and Mahesh known as 'Brahma-Puranas', 'Vaishnava-Puranas', and 'Shaiva-Puranas'.

There are also a large number of 'Upa-Puranas' ('Lesser Puranas') associated with other Gods and Goddesses. In some cases, however. the diving line between 'Maha-Puranas' and 'Upa-Puranas' is rather thin. For instance, the devotees of goddess Durga consider the 'Devibhagwat Purana' as 'Maha-Purana', even as others classify it as 'Upa-Purana'. Apart from these god-specific 'Puranas', there are also a number of 'Sthala-Puranas' describing some miraculous events connected with particulaly holy places and deities installed there. For instance, as described earlier, there is 'Guruvaupura-Purana' which dwells upon the mythology associated with the idol of Vishnu-Naraina' located at Guruvayoor in present day Kerala.

Over-all, the Purana's are a store-house of magnificent Hindu mythologies through which they throw light on morality and ethics besides the nature of the universe. Mythology is a part of every religion, but the rich mythology of Hinduism, complied through centuries, is unmatched in the world. The very fact that there are so many of these, connected with so many events and places, goes to show the richness of Hindu mythology. For practising Hindus, there are numerous religious practices in day-to-day life which are rooted in one Puranic mythology or the other. In that sense 'Puranas" are very much live, setting the tone of Hindu religions life even today. Through simple stories of reward and punishment, good and bad, the 'Puranas' act as guide books of righteous conduct on the part of common Hindus.

Apart from regular 'Pooja', that is, worship of God in the form on an icon at home, observance of numerous festivals is very much a part of Hindu religious life. Festivals are observed by total or partial fasting, bathing in holy rivers and prayers before deities seeking boons for worldly life combined with a dose of entertainment. There are such a large number of such pious occasions that devout Hindu men and women keep celebrating one or the other almost throughout the year. And all these holy days or festivals are based on and derived from one Puranic story or the other.

One of the most widely celebrated Hindu festivals is Durga Pooja, that is, Worship of Goddess Durga or Devi. It is celebrated with great gusto and devotion particularly in Bengal, Bihar and Assam in Eastern and Gujarat in Western India. Images of the goddess are installed at public places for collective worship by devotees. For nine days during what is known as 'Navaratra', many ardent devotees perform private worship of Devi at home by reciting "Durga Sapta-shati' every morning ceremonially and fasting partially. The festival celeberates the destruction of the ferocious demon 'Mahisasura'. who had terrorised the 'Devas' or righteous inhabitants of heaven, by goddess Durga. also known as 'Mahisasura -Marclini' after this event. Where does this mythological episode come from? Evidenly from the, Puranas.

Although it is narrated in several 'Puranas' with minor differences, the main story comes from the 'Markandeya Purana', one of the six 'Brahma-Puranas'. It is also described at some length in 'Devi Bhagawata Purana'. The story is like this :-

F or about a hundred years, 'Devas' and 'Asuras' (Demons) were engaged in a grim war which ended in the defeat of the 'Devas'. The 'Devas' approached Gods Shiva and Vishnu for rescue. It was out of the anger of Shiva and Vishnu that goddess Devi or Durga was born as the embodiment of 'Shakti'. She began the fight against the demon 'Mahisasura' by her "loud roar" with a defying laugh. In the final battle, the Mother of the worlds, Devi, also called Chandika, kills the demon Mahisasura by cutting off his head with her sword. Through the destruction of Mahisasura who was evil incarnate, the Devi thus rescued the 'Devas', and saved the universe from destruction.

In the prayer that is offered to the Mother Goddess or Devi in praise of her great act, all her essential qualities are worshipfully highlighted. She is 'the origin of the universe, the resort of all, the primordial Prakriti. . .. the Supreme Vidya which is the cause of liberation'. Many devotees of Devi or Durga recite the prayer not only during the nine days of Durga Puja ('Navaratra'), but part of it regularly in course of their daily 'Pooja.'

That would show the over all impact of Puranic mythology on the religious practices of Hindus. The 'Puranas', it may be noted, are specifically mythological books, presenting one coherent body of mythology as against the Vedic mythology scattered through hymns, rituals and philosophy. In that sense, while the Vedas constitute the rock foundation of Hinduism, the 'Puranas' form the superstructure more visible in the day-to-day life of practising Hindus.

(b) The Epics: Ramayan and Mahabharata:

With all their wide range and sweep, the 'Puranas' cannot match the ancient epics-Ramayana and Mahabharata - which are the most important texts broadly coming under the category of 'Smritis'. From the point of view of their impact on modern Hindu society, the epics far over-shadow and out-shine the 'Puranas' and other constituent texts of the 'Smritis'. The great Sanskrit 'Ramayana', attributed to Rishi Valmiki, contains 24,000 Verses in all, composed in accordance with the rules of Vedic poetry. 'Mahabharata' is the second great Sanskrit epic attributed to sage Vyasa containing one lac verses. They are generally regarded as part of India's post-Vedic Pre-history.

Professional historians keep debating about or rather guessing about their dates and authorship according to their own predilections or pre-conceived notions. But from the point of view of Hindu beliefs and practices, historicity of the epics is hardly of any significance. It is their contents and ethical and moral values emerging from them that account for their scriptural importance to Hindus. K.M. Munshi summed it up when he observed: "The Ramayana and Mahabharata underwent recessions from time to time and became the one irrestible creative force which has shaped the collective spirit of the people."

In the hierarchy of sacred texts, the epics Ramayana and Mahabharata are placed well below the Vedas (including the Upanishads) which stand at the top. The epics do not prescribe any overt rules of conduct or lay down any edicts for the people to follow. Through simple narration of two great events at different points of time in the past - the Rama - Ravana clash and Kaurava - Pandava war - they bring out the eternal principles of morality and ethical conduct valid for the whole of humanity. Through gripping accounts of interaction between the principal characters, the epics highlight the moral issues of right and wrong, good and evil, so vitally relevant to human society. And since they come in the form of interesting human stories, Ramayana and Mahabharata have an instant appeal for the people. As such, the epics have impacted the life and conduct of the common mass of Hindus much more than the Vedic rituals and Upanishadic philosophy which are hardly intelligible to them.

It is more so in case of Ramayana. The pre-eminence of Ramayana in the galaxy of sacred books is not because of its historicity or the literary beauty of Valmiki's 'Shlokas' in lucid style. It is so because its central character or hero, Rama, has come to occupy the centre-stage in the common religious perception of Hindus. And yet, it was not so when the original Ramayan was created in Sanskrit by Rishi Valmiki in the hoary past. Paradoxically, the Rama legend came to its full glory during a period when Hinduism itself was under grave challenge during Muslim rule. The dark period of severe Islamist onslaught against Hinduism brought forth a number of illustrious 'Bhakti' poets who glorified the hero of Valmiki's Ramayana as the God Supreme, that is, Vedanta's "Param Brahman".

In the literary works of such eminent saint poets like Kabir Das and Raidas, Rama figures not as the 'Sagun' (Manifest) Rama of Valmiki's epic but as the 'Nirgun' (formless) God Supreme. To them, Rama was not just the divine son of Raja Dashrath who demolished the evil Ravana but the all pervasive formless God or the Supreme Soul of Vedanta. In other words, the name Rama no longer remained a proper name referring to a particular godly, mythological or historical figure but became a synonym of or substitute for the term 'Ishwara' signifying the God Supreme Himself. This transformation of Rama into a generic name denoting the Supreme God is profusely reflected in the works of a number of saint poets like Namdeo, Maluk Das, Apa Saheb and others, besides Kabir Das and Raidas.

An eloquent expression of complete identification of Rama with the formless Supreme God or 'Ishwara' is found in the 'Gurubani' (sacred words) of Sikh Gurus. So much so that in the holy 'Guru Granth Sahib' the name Rama occurs as many as 2400 times as identical with the Supreme God or 'Param Brahman'. Sri 'Guru Granth Sahib', it may be noted, is a collection of sacred poetic words of Sikh Gurus from Guru Nanak onwards as well of saints like Namdeo, Ramananda, Kabir Das, Raidas and others compiled by the fifth Guru Sri Arjun Deo in the year 1604. Thus Rama got enshrined as a synonym of 'Nirgun' (Formless) God Supreme in the holy book of this great religion of Hindu family.

But the emergence of 'Sagun' (Manifest) Rama of Valmiki's Ramayan as the most worshipped god of the Hindus in general was to wait till another great saint poet - Goswami Tulsi Das - appeared on the scene. The grand story of Rama as an incarnation of Vishnu and his epic clash with Ravana, the embodiment of evil, was well preserved in Valmiki's Sanskrit magnum opus and Kamban Ramayan of the South. But the saga of Rama as the embodiment of eternal values, of all that is good for humanity, did not become so hugely reverential and worshipful for the Hindu masses until Tulsi Das came out with his version of Ramayan in the 16th Century.

Inspired by Swami Ramanand, who was committed to ward off the onslaught of Islamism during the peak of Muslim rule, Tulsi Das undet-took to reach the glorious Rama story to every Hindu house-hold in his own way. Although he was an erudite Sanskrit scholar in his own right, he chose to render the story of Ramayana in simple Awadhi dialect of Hindi so as to be easily accessible to the common people. Sitting on the banks of the holy river Ganga in Varanasi under the patronage of Swami Ramananda, Tulsidas wrote his monumental book - 'Ram Charit Manas'- in the form of lucid couplets which had an instant appeal.

It may be recalled that Gautam Buddha had centuries before used the common language of the people of Magadh among whom be lived and preached, which was 'Prakrit'. And it was from 'Prakrit' that 'Pali' language developed in which all early Buddhist scriptures were written. And yet, Buddhism eventually spread not only in large parts of India but also in South East and East Asia. Some what in the same way, the Rama Story as depicted in Tulsi's 'Ram Charit Manas' gripped the Hindu mind in the whole of India as never before.

All basic Hindu scriptures including the epics were written in Sanskrit which the common people could not access. The rendering of Ramayana in easily understandable Hindi made Rama a house-hold god worshipped by every practising Hindu. The principal characters of Ramayana, epitomizing the obedience of a son, devotion of a wife, affection and sacrifice of a brother, got embossed on the mind of the people as ideals. They have come to be the role models of the common people even today.

The context and time in which Tulsi Das wrote his Ramayana had a lot to do with its immense popularity among the Hindu masses. Hinduism was under severe challenge from over-powering Islamism during the height of Muslim rule. The Hindus were down-cast and feeling utterly helpless in saving their faith and identity. In such a grim backdrop, Tulsi's Ramayana brought to the fore the heroic role of divine Rama in demolishing the forces of evil and establishing the supremacy of 'Dharma'. In an oblique reference to Islamist aggression, Tulsi's 'Manas' conveys the message that whenever 'dharma' is put to harm and demonic forces are on the ascendance, God appears in different incarnations and relieves the people of their sufferings. ('Ram Charit Manas' - Bal Kand, - 120). This was a replication of Lord Krishna's famous observation in Gita to the same effect.

Needless to say, such an emphatic assertion of God's immanence and readiness to come to their rescue in times of grave threat sustained the Hindu masses during the Islamic rule and reinforced their determination to stick to their faith. It became a great source of sustenance in all their tribulations, religious or otherwise.

The great impact of Ramayan on the religious life and practices of Hindus has continued down to this day. The two major festivals-Vijaya Dashmi (Dashara) and Deepawali (festival of lights) celebrated by Hindus all over the country are derived from the story of Ramayana. While Vijaya Dashmi celeberates Rama's Victory over Ravana, symbolizing the victory of good over evil, Deepawali represents his triumphant return to Ayodhya after 14 years. 'Rama Katha' or the story of Rama is the most common denominator of religious discourses among rural people. The couplets of Ramayana are liberally quoted by village pundits and wise old men to distinguish between right and wrong and lay emphasis on ethical conduct.

Even among the more enlightened Hindus, the story of Ramayan is analysed and deliberated upon with religious fervour. Quite a number of religious minded people recite some couplets of Ramayan as part of their daily 'Pooja' in their homes. Hanuman, the other great Godly character of Ramayan, is widely worshipped by Hindus in day to day life. There are any number of faithfuls who begin their day with recital of 'Hanuman Chalisa' created by Tulsi Das in devotion to the God Hanuman.

Vedic rituals are, of course, still adhered to at life-cycle events like births, marriages, deaths etc. Some sophisticated believers recite the Vedic 'Gayatri Mantra' in course of their 'Pooja' before starting their day. But the worship of Lord Rama in some form or the other has come to be by far the most common form of Hindu worship. Mere Chanting of the name Rama, such as, 'Hare Rama', 'Hare Rama', as many times as possible, singly or collectively, is a commonly practiced form of worship. It may be sorrowfully recalled that when Mahatma Gandhi, the greatest universalist of modern age, fell to the assassin's bullets, the last words that he uttered were "Hay Rama". That is a measure of the oversize impact of Ramayana on Hindu life as well as of complete identification of Rama with the God Supreme or 'Param Brahman.'

Like Ramayana, Mahabharata is another epic story of the eternal conflict between the right and wrong, good and evil. It is the story of the marathon war between the Pandavas and Kurus or Kaurvas, the former representing the cause of the right and the latter symbolizing the wrong. And like the Ramayana again, the right or the just comes out victorious against the wrong or the unjust. But from the point of view of their value as scriptures, the similarity ends here. In Ramayana, the hero or the principal character - Rama - himself comes out as an incarnation of God. In Mahabharata, on the other hand, divinity does not lie in the hero namely Arjun or other Pandava brothers representing the right cause. It is Krishna, the side character of the epic as charioteer of Arjun in the great war, who is the God incarnate. Ramayana is a sacred text as the life story of Rama, the God incarnate. In case of Mahabharata, it is not the account of the conflict between the Pandavas and Kauravas and the great war between them that is sacred. It is Lord Krishna's solemn observations made in course of the war that are believed to be divine gospel. And these are compiled in the gem of a scriptural text known as the 'Gita'.

'Smriti' : (c) : The Gita

There is nothing in the labyrinthine story of Mahabharata to count it among the sacred texts of Hindus except the godly role of the side character Krishna culminating in the eloquent Gita. If the Gita is taken out of it, the epic will remain no more than a part of India's pre or proto history with a mix of mythology and ethics.

Here again, professional historians keep debating about the date and authorship of Gita, as in the case of epics as a whole. According to some, Gita was not composed by Rishi Vyasa, who is believed to be the author of Mahabharata as a whole, but was a later addition to the epic. As observed earlier in case of the epics, the historicity or exact authorship of the Gita is immaterial in view of the immense spiritual value of its contents. Suffice it to say that Bhagwadgita stands out as the epitome of Hindu system of thought and bedrock of Hindu faith.

The Gita contains 78 'shlokas' (verses) divided into 18 chapters and stands out as a compact book of gospel on its own. Its only link with the Mahabarata story is that it is supposed to be the record of conversation between Lord Krishna and Arjuna while standing at the head of a large Pandava army facing a larger Kaurava armed force right in the battle field of Kurukshetra; But in the entire conversation, there is hardly any overt reference to strategy of war in the impending battle between the two opposing forces. Instead, the Krishna-Arjuna dialogue, which constitutes the Gita, is all about the highest principles of philosophy, metaphysics, and process of creation and means of ultimate salvation of man. On the other hand, the 12th book of Mahabharata entitled 'Shanti-Parva', supposed to contain the observations of Bhishma Pitamaha as he lay dying on a pile of arrows, is largely about a king's duties and strategies of war. It would appear, therefore, that as a sacred text of eternal value, the Gita is not an appendage of Mahabharata but rather the Mahabharata is an appendage of Gita.

Apart from the scriptural value of its message, there is another significant feature of Gita which greatly enhances its sanctity as a holy book of Hindus. It is only Gita and not the Mahabharata as such, which eloquently describes the transcendental form of Lord Krishna as the primal cause of all things, the creator and absorber of all things, the repository of the entire universe and the God of all Gods. This was revealed to Arjuna by Lord Krishna himself in the middle of the battle field (chapter 11).

In fact, the entire teaching of Gita is in the form of a lecture delivered by a teacher to his pupil. It would, thus appear to be more in the nature of a revealed text. In this sense, there is some justification for regarding the Gita as a part of the 'Shruti' (revealed word of God), as Hindus generally believe. On the other hand, the Mahabharata, shorn of the Gita, has never been considered to be more than a part of the 'Smritis' (the remembered text) like the 'Puranas'. That would place Gita above the Mahabharata bereft of it in the hierarchy of Hindu scriptures.

It would be appropriate at this stage to touch upon the quintessence of Gita as a Hindu scripture. It would appear that the Gita dispenses with the primacy of rituals prescribed in the Vedic Samhitas. But it sticks to and in fact reinforces the essence of Hindu theism, which is belief in and realization of 'Param

Brahman', the absolute God who alone is true. And that is the end-product and quintessence of the holistic teachings of Vedas, in their wider meaning, culminating in the message of the Upanishads. Every other teaching contained in the Vedas represents a stage in the course of man's progress towards realization of the Absolute God or Supreme Soul. For, while man's body is perishable, his soul is indestructible and eternal and its ultimate destination is union with the Supreme Soul or 'Param Brahan'. That sums up the basics of Hinduism.

With its compactness, directness and simplicity, devoid of the trappings of complicated rituals, Gita has come to be regarded as God's own gospel by Hindus, somewhat in the same way as the Bible is regarded by Christians and the Quran by Muslims. It is under such a belief that any number of practising Hindus religiously recite selected 'Shlokas' (verses) of Gita as part of their regular 'Pooja'.

While Gita accepts the vedantic or upanishadic view of Absolute God as the formless supreme Soul, it also says that God incarnates himself as manifest ('Saguna') God from time to time to redeem humanity and uphold righteousness. This has been clearly brought out in Lord Krishna's famous proclamation before Arjuna as follows :-

"Whenever there is any decline of 'dharma' I am born in order to uplift 'dharma'.

To save the righteous, destroy the evil ones and re-establish 'dharma, , 1 create myself from age to age." (chapter 4-7/8)

This categorical declaration of God's incarnation from time to time reinforced devotion to 'Saguna' (manifest) God, which had ever been widely practised by Hindus. More importantly, Gita's positive message of God's intervention to save 'dharma' in times of need struck a sympathetic chord in the Hindu heart.

For over seven hundred years of Islamic and British rule, the Hindus were at the receiving end and Hindu dharma under grave threat. To the Hindus, struggling to retain their faith and identity under adverse situations, Gita's above "Shloka' was a beacon of hope. Tulsi Das replicated it in his 'Ram Charit Manas' when Hinduism was facing decline during the heyday of Muslim rule. Needless to say, it has ever served as an elixir to rejuvinate and sustain Hinduism from 'age to age'.

As word here about the exact meaning or connotation of the term 'dharma'. Commentators on Gita have generally interpreted the term to denote righteousness or moral correctness. But the word 'dharma' as used in common parlance is taken to mean religion, pure and simple. In fact, there is no other proper word in Sanskrit or Hindi to denote religion except 'dharma'. In popular perception, therefore, this 'Shloka' of Gita is taken literally to mean that whenever the (Hindu) religion declines or is threatened by evil forces, God incarnates himself to rescue it. Metaphorically, that may be taken to explain the miracle of survival of Hinduism through some of the most severe assaults on it in course of its long and chequered history. The Hindus generally seem to think so.

It is another matter that the interpretation of the word 'Dharma' to indicate righteousness in a wider sense is also valid. That way, 'dharma' is also the word for duty, as in the case of 'Swadharma' or "Rajdharma'.

This semantic ambivalence or ambiguity about the word "dharma', however, need not be stretched too far, because in the ultimate analysis, religion, righteousness and morally correct duty mingle into one, to defend which, according to Gita, God incarnates himself from time to time.

Even as Gita upholds the theory of incarnation of God as a saviour of 'dharma' and destroyer of evil, it also depicts the all-pervading, omnipotent and omniscient 'Param Brahman' as a most lovable manifest (Saguna) God in the form of Lord Krishna. All that he wants of his worshippers is total self-surrender and love. This has been beautifully brought out in Lord Krishna's address to Arjuna as a manifest (Saguna) God recorded in Gita :-

"I am the father of this world, its mother, its grandfather.

I am the object of knowledge, the purifier, the syllable "Om"...............

I am Rig, Sama, Yajur (the three Vedas) as well. (chapter 9 - 17)

I am the soul which resides in the heart of all things.

I am the beginning, the middle and the end (chapter 10 - 20)

I am the abode of the immortal Param Brahman, of 'Amrit' (Ambrosia or Nectar) of eternal righteousness and total bliss." (chapter 14 - 27)

After describing himself thus, in person, Lord Krishna tells Arjuna : -

"Abandon all the ways of religion and take refuge in me *alone.*

By emancipating you from all sins, I shall lead you to *"Moksha" (Salvation), so don't be sad".* (chapter 18 - 66)

The sheer grandeur of Lord Krishna's exhortation so grandly captured in Gita laid the foundation of the intensely devotional "Bhaktl" movement of the middle or 'dark ages' represented by such dedicated Krishna devotees as Soor Das,

Meera Bal and others. It continues to sway any number of Krishna devotees not only in India but also internationally through the ISCON (International Society of Krishna Consciousness). This form of worship of Lord Krishna as manifest God with complete surrender and pure love takes away the burden of performing rites and rituals. Thereby, it makes worship of God fairly simple and has led to the spread of Krishna cult beyond the frontiers of India.

This way, the Gita has significantly impacted the Hindu mode of worship. But the reach of Gita extends well beyond the sphere of pure worship. It is actually in the field of worldly action that Gita has made a singular contribution to Hindu thought and activism. It has given a philosophy of 'karma' or worldly action, as opposed to in-action, which raises it above the mundane, almost to the level of worship. 'Work is worship' is a well-known motto of modern life. Gita has given a new meaning to it by attaching a degree of sacredness to work done in performance of one's duty. This is the core message that lord Krishna himself gave to Arjuna in the battle feild of Kurukshetra recorded in the Gita. When Arjuna, torn by mental conflict in fighting against his own Kins and elders, refused to join the battle, lord Krishna told him in clear terms : -

"If you do not fight this 'dharmayuddha' (righteous war) you will be failing to do your legitimate duty ('swadharma'), therby losing fame and sinning". (chapter 2 -33)

In other words, Gita affirms that to fight against injustice and evil is a man's bounden duty and to flinch from it is sinful. There cannot be a more categorical assertion of what may be termed as the doctrine of 'Karmvad', that is positive activism in the cause of justice and righteousness. This core message of Gita has inspired the people of India at all times and continues to do so even to-day. It deprecates inaction or passivity in the face of evil as outright sinful. It is relevant for the whole of humanity and for all times.

In the sphere of religion, the impact of Gita's message is clearly discernible in the works of 'Bhakti' poets like Kabir Das, Rai Das and Tulsi Das to resist the rising tide of Islamism during Muslim rule. In modem times, Bal Gangadhar Tilak and Mahatma Gandhi interpreted the Gita's doctorine of 'Karmavad' to inspire and strengthen the Indian nationalist Movement and freedom struggle against British rule. The Gita's message of positive activism was the principal source of inspiration for revolutionary freedom-fighters who sacrificed their lives in the cause of freedom. In fact, many revolutionary freedom-fighters carried a copy of Gita with them as primal source book of inspiration for their work.

But Gita's message of positive activism was best interpreted and put into practice by the tallest of illustrious Indians in modern age - Mahatma Gandhi. His methodology of 'Satyagraha' as a potent mode of resistance to any amount of injustice could easily be traced back to Gita's edict of action or 'Karmavada'. Gandhi's technique of 'Satyagrah' is a unique programme of direct but non-violent social action by people tormented by any kind of unjust and evil dispensation anywhere in the world.

The Mahatma has himself explained at the close of his famous autobiography how his commitment to truth led him to political activism. He observes - "My uniform experience has convinced me that there is no other God than Truth.....To see the universal and all-pervading spirit of Truth face to face, one must be able to love the meanest of creation as oneself. And a man who aspires after that can not afford to keep out of any field of life. That is why my devotion to Truth has drawn me into the field of politics". The imprint of Gita's 'mantra' of 'karma' is clearly reflected in the ring and tone of Mahatma Gandhi's words explaining his political activism.

Gita's 'mantra' of action or 'karmavada' does not stop at that. It upgrades 'karma', that is action in performance of one's duty, to the level of 'yoga' terming it as 'karma yoga'. In other words, it makes 'yoga' of action a part of man's godward endeavour, that is a means of his ultimate salvation. "Yoga' in this sense is not the same as the 'yoga' system of Indian philosophy, In Gita, 'yoga' is taken to denote a disciplined and stable state of mind totally detached from the vagaries of senses and emotions. 'Karmayoga' as a medium of realization of God or the ultimate Truth, as Gandhi says, is all about this kind of completely detached action or performance of duty.

Gita does recognize the 'yoga' of 'Sanyasa' (renunciation) as a means of realization of God. In keeping with the upanishadic concept of knowledge as a means of being one with God, Gita upholds that 'sanyasis' do realize God through the 'yoga' of knowledge (gyan yoga). Gita terms it as 'karmasanyasa'. But for common man, 'yoga' of action ('karmayoga') is better than 'yoga' of renunciation ('karmasanyasa') because it is easier. For man has to engage in action in normal course even to sustain his body. Gita thus places action above renunciation, which defines the Hindu religious thought and practice.

But what about the Hindu belief in action resulting in man's re-birth to reap the fruits of his 'karma', good or bad ? How can man be liberated from the mortal cycle of re-birth and suffering by indulging in action? Gita's answer to that is the remarkable doctrine of 'Nishkamakarma', that is totally detached action, which is an unique- contribution of Gita and Hinduism to the world. 'Nishkama Karma' means action done without any lust for its fruits leaving the result in the hands of God. This has been beautifully summed up in Gita's 'Shloka'-

"Karmanyeva Dhikaraste
Ma phaleshu kadachana"

("Thu art entitled to work but not to its result".) (chapter 2 - 47) Mahatma Gandhi has termed it as 'Anasakti yoga' (yoga of detachment).

According to it, a man can continue with his worldly life, like Raja Janak, and do everything which had to be done without scarifying his religious aspirations. The only condition is that he must not expect any profit from his worldly action. This is perfectly in keeping with the basic Hindu (Upanishadic) view that man's desire leads to his re-birth and suffering. Once desire is conquered while at the same time performing all worldly duties perfectly well, the door of ultimate salvation, that is final liberation of the soul from the cycle of transmigration into human bodies, is opened. By giving up desire to reap the fruits of his worldly action and doing his work without the thought of 'I did it', a man can realize his highest religious aspiration of being one with God. That is Gita's doctrine of 'Nishkama Karma' as an integral part of 'Karma Yoga' or 'Anasakti Yoga'. Through the practice of 'Nishkama Karma' or detached action, man could live his life fully in this world and secure his other world also.

As a Hindu religious scripture, Gita lays emphasis on this-wordly action by man without jeopardizing his ultimate salvation. As mentioned earlier, it was a great source of inspiration for nationalist political activism in the initial stages of India's freedom struggle. Even for common man in modern world, Gita's doctrine of 'Nishkama Karma' or detached action is relevant and practicable to an extent. A certain degree of detachment in doing one's duty even in professional life is not only possible but also beneficial. For, it brings about peace of mind from a sense of having done one's duty to the best of one's capacity without being much too obsessed with the result. It thereby shields the doer from both wild expectations and fear of grave disappointment which could be counter-productive.

Here is a real life story of an ambitious young man aspiring for reaching great heights in his professional career. As long as he was seized with wild desires while doing his work, he met with successive failures inspite of all his efforts tinged with too much infatuation with his goal. So much so that he once even thought of committing suicide. Ultimately, his father, an old professional himself, came to his rescue. Though not a particularly religious person himself, with only rudimentary idea of the Hindu scriptures, the old man advised his son to carry on with his efforts in a detached way without being obsessed with his goal leaving the result in the hands of God. The young man readily grasped the idea and started putting it into practice as best as he could. And the result was nothing short of a miracle. His professional work done with a degree of detachment without being bothered about the result started bearing fruit. It brought him peace of mind and emotional satisfaction, apart from much better work-performance and vastly improved out-come, which eventually brightened his career.

That was 'Nishkama Karma' or detached action in practical life. That way Gita's 'Karma-Vada' is not merely a religious doctrine. It might as well serve as a guide book for successful professional life in modern world.

29

Special Features of Hinduism

I. Religious Tolerance

Hinduism can be identified by some unique characteristics which distinguish it from other organized religions of the world. The most important and visible distinguishing mark of Hinduism is its extraordinary tolerance of diverse faiths, philosophies and practices that it has come in contact with. It is this open arm and eclectical approach of Hinduism towards other religions that has made Hindu India a safe haven for followers of diverse faiths right from ancient to modern times. As dealt with in an earlier chapter, the Israelis came, the Syrian Christians, Arab Muslims, Zoroastrians and Bahai's came from time to time and lived in peace with the Hindu people. The ten lost tribes of Israelis are believed to have mingled and merged with the people of northern India. The Syrian Christians and early Arah Muslims came and built their Churches and Mosques, practised their religion and even converted many locals without any opposition from the Hindu Society.

That was, of course, before political Islam, as distinguished from Islam as a pure faith, entered India with 'sword in hand' in the form of Mahmud Ghazni beginning the 11th century. But that is part of another story which has been briefly dealt with in chapter eleven. That incidentally brings out the sharp contrast between the outstanding religious tolerance of Hinduism and extreme intolerance of politico-religious ideology of Islamism.

In any case, the jarring religious intolerance of politico-Islam or Islamism which came to India with "fire and slaughter" could not interrupt or overwhelm the symphony of religious toleration which has ever been the hall-mark of Hinduism. That is the most remarkable fact of Hindu ethos and history which has not been properly understood and appreciated.

One is apt to think some times that toleration is a cover for weakness or passivity of Hinduism in the face of aggressive intolerance of other religions. It is not; on the other hand, it is a measure of supreme self-confidence of Hindu people in their strong spiritual roots capable of coping with any amount of aggression by intolerant religions. For, apart from being the oldest living religion of the world having survived through the vicissitudes of history and ravages of time, Hinduism represents the basic human urge to discover the ultimate reality in whatever way one chooses. Since the belief in and connectivity with the ultimate reality, call it by whatever name like the Supreme Soul, Primal Source of all creation, or God, is the universal principle underlying all religions, there is no real contradiction between one religion and another. It is this perception inherent in Hinduism which is the source of its remarkable tolerance of other religions.

In fact, such an understanding of the basics of religion is fostered by Hindu scriptures based on spiritual endeavours and insights of our sages and seens through the ages. All apostles of

Hinduism from ancient to modern times have proclaimed it from time to time. Swami Ram Krishna said it in so many words when he observed that it is the same God towards whom all are directing their steps, though along different paths. Hinduism thus acknowledges that there are many paths along which man may seek God and experience spiritual fulfillment. This is the core of Hindu religiousity. It is ingrained in Hindu psyche. And this is the real basis of utmost tolerance of Hinduism towards all faiths.

This all embracing universalistic religious paradigm of Hinduism enables it to accept diverse faiths and practices with perfect ease. It is not a sign of passivity or weakness but of courage of conviction of Hindu people in their interaction with followers of other religions. Hinduism is the only religion in the world which has enough width and space to accommodate other faiths without compromising with its distinct identity.

This apparently sweeping assertion calls for a little explanation here. Christian nations of the western world today also claim to practice religious toleration in the name of what they call 'multi-culturism'. That is, they tolerate followers of other faiths to live and practice their own religion in their predominantly Christian countries. But there is a subtle difference here between *toleration* and *acceptance*. While Christian countries *tolerate* non-Christians, the church as such does not accept other faiths as true. On the other hand, Hinduism and Hindu India accept all other faiths as true, being diverse paths leading to the same God. It is in this sense that Hinduism stands out alone as the most tolerant religion in the world.

This has been best expressed by Mahatma Gandhi in an article in his paper, the "Young India". Elaborating upon his Hindu identity, the Mahatma observed: *"Believing as I do in the influence of heredity, being born in a Hindu family, I have remained a Hindu....... On examination, I have found it to be the most tolerant of all religions known to me. Its freedom from dogma makes a forcible appeal to me in as much as it gives the votary the largest scope for self-expression. Not being an exclusive religion, it enables the followers of that faith not merely to respect all other religions, but it also enables them to admire and assimilate whatever may be good in the other faiths."*

That says it all about the unique feature of religious toleration, or rather acceptance, in-grained in Hinduism. It has no central orthodoxy based on a single book or a sole prophet as in the case of Islam. Its tenets are not frozen edicts of a frozen past, but live principles of righteous living being ever renewed and renewable. Its openness to new ideas and aspiration for universality instead of exclusivity sets it apart from other religions which identify their followers by their belief in particular historical events, personalities and revelations. Hinduism is not much concerned with the origin or history of ideas but with their truth and validity established through direct experience of seekers. It encourages its followers to explore all avenues that could lead to a realization of the Divine. It signifies a religious system with many paths for such realization. That is the secret of the marvelous religious toleration or acceptance of Hinduism.

In the present age of alarming rise in religious conflicts or 'clash of civilizations', Hinduism is an oasis of peace and reconciliation. The Hindu world-view of pluralism and respect for diverse modes of worship presents a model for reconciliation of religious conflicts the world over. The Christian drive for evangelization and the Muslim bid for Islamisation create situations for clash of religions. Hinduism on the other hand, does not call for conversion of people to any one creed. It has always sought to enlighten people rather than to convert them, thus enabling every religion to maintain its distinct identity and religious practices. Hindus could that way he taken as role models for followers of other more rigid religions involved in bitter religious or sectarian conflicts. For Hindus have no problems with non-Hindus. It is they who have problems because of their rigid orthodoxy. But Hinduism has taken them in its stride for centuries and survived inspite of their sustained proselytizing efforts. *And it will continue to do so.*

II. Experimentation, Renewal and Freedom

Significantly enough, Mahatma Gandhi's autobiography is entitled "The story of my Experiments with Truth". The title is pregnant with profound significance. It brings to light another distinguishing feature of Hinduism. It is the Hindu readiness to continually experiment as a means of discovering the spiritual truth in the manner of scientific enquiry. In dedicating his life to experimenting with truth which he regarded as God, the Mahatma was essentially following the Hindu tradition of experimentation. For Hinduism has always been experimenting with and assimilating fresh ideas as a means of connecting with the ultimate Truth or God Supreme. It is this continual quest for Spiritual truth as demonstrated through direct experience which has renewed Hinduism from time to time and kept it abreast of the times. As Hinduism is not bound by the edicts of a single book and commandments of a sole prophet, renewal of its tradition has always come from sages and saints in every age who base their pronouncements on direct experience of the divine. (From Rishi Valmiki, Vyas, Adi Shankaracharya down to Swami Rama Krishna Paramhans, Vivekananda and Sri Aurobindo) That essentially accounts for the survival of this oldest of known religions even in this post-modern age.

A constantly evolving and flowering religion, as a synthesis of many experiences and streams of thought, Hinduism is a complex but most liberal religion which gives its followers utmost freedom of religious practice. In that sense, it is the most dogma-free religion in the world. The Hindu scriptures based on the experiments and insights of sages and seers, as said above, serve primarily not as order book but as guide books for individual seekers. Hinduism as such allows complete freedom to each individual to seek and connect with God according to his own understanding in his own way. This freedom is clearly noticeable in the immense variety of worship which the Hindus practise in day-to-day life. Many people worship their idol at home. Most people worship images of many Gods simultaneously, either in temples or at home, believing them to be different manifestations of the one God Supreme. Some worship God by chanting His name ('Hare Rama, Hare Krishna') many times while some worship by offering items of food and money before the deity.

Hinduism admits of innumerable ways of worship and communion with God in accordance with the spiritual evolution of man. A Hindu has utmost freedom to communicate with God physically by worshipping his image or idol, mentally by meditating upon his form or image and spiritually through complete silence of the mind in fusion with the invisible and infinite Divine Soul or 'Param Brahman'. For Hindus, all these forms of worship and communication with God are valid and have their own relevance in the spiritual evolution of man.

Finally, some may not worship God in any form, and root for other, more worldly tangible things like money, sensory pleasure, name, fame, power, etc. Hinduism does not reject them, punish them or throw them out of the fold. There is no concept of heresy or blasphemy in Hinduism, for it is not governed by an organized religious establishment like the Roman Catholic Church. Nor is there any system of Fatwah being issued by Islamic Seminaries or Mullahs against heretics and those who chart out an independent course in defiance of the established faith. For, apart from its wide and universalistic canvas, Hinduism has no organized establishment like the

Christian Church or even the Institution of Ulemas to regulate its followers. Adi Shankaracharya did establish four 'Pithas' or religious Seminaries in four corners of the Country as beacons of Hindu faith. But they were meant only to enlighten the Hindus on the basics of their faith, and not to dictate them to stick to a particular course or to punish them for deviating from it.

Wonder of wonders, Hinduism had space enough to accommodate even the out-right hedonistic philosophy of *Charavaka* with clear irreligious undertones. According to the Charavaka School of thought, all religious observances and morality were futile. A man should make the best use of life by enjoying it to the full regardless of all religious and ethical considerations. This view is blatantly expressed in the following couplet attributed to Charavaka : -

"As long as he lives, a man should live happily and drink ghee, even though he runs into debt. For when the body is turned into ashes, How can there be return to life?"

Not only that. A certain amount of materialist and irreligious undercurrent is also noticeable in two of the most famous Hindu classics - Kautilya's 'Arthashastra' and 'Vatsyayan's 'Kama Sutra'. Kautilya was of course a political strategist who has dwelt upon the temporal or non-religious topic of statecraft. But Vatsyayan was a great sage who was totally absorbed in contemplation of the Divine when he wrote his famous book - the 'Kama Sutra'. In the words of Leo Markun, "Vatsyana, the author of 'Kama Sutra', was not a hack writer .... He wrote his 'Aphorisms of Love' in high seriousness, and with no feeling of shame". And he wrote his classic on sex some time during the Gupta period which historians term as 'Golden Age' of Hindu India.

Being a sage himself, Vatsyayan beautifully synthesized sex life with 'Dharma' (religious piety or righteousness). He conceived of a trinity of 'Dharma', 'Artha' (Wealth) and 'Kama' (Sexual pleasure) as essential ingredients of a meaningful life. Rejecting the argument that sexual pleasures were obstacles to practice of 'Dharma', he observed. "The pleasures are as necessary for the well-being of the body as food and drink. They are consequently equally important". But he adds a note of caution, "we should indulge in pleasures, of course, in *moderation and with caution*". Can there be a more positive affirmation of freedom to enjoy the pleasures of worldly life coming from a religious seer?

And yet, neither Charavaka nor Vatsyayan were discarded by Hinduism as heretics or renegades. They are an integral part of the liberal Hindu tradition which allows a person to choose his way of life in his own discretion without his faith coming in the way. Hinduism does not bind him to any rigid religious regime, leaving him free to live his life fully in accordance with his own best judgement. Taken as a way of life, Hinduism is thus the freeest religious tradition in the world, giving its followers complete freedom to live their worldly life in their own way. But this does not mean that it supports permissiveness or incorrect way of life. For with freedom comes responsibility and Hinduism clearly suggests that every one is responsible for the result of his actions. That is, 'as you sow, so you reap'.

The Hindu scriptures repeatedly emphasize that man has to reap the consequences of his actions, good or bad. Through mythological stories and, aphorisms, the 'Puranas' and epics make it amply clear that wrong actions inevitably lead to suffering. Whoever chooses a wrong and immoral way of life has to suffer from its harmful consequences either in this life or in the next. It may be noted that belief in transmigration of soul and re-birth are essential ingredients of Hindu faith indelibly imprinted on the Hindu psyche. However ostensibly rationalist a Hindu may be, the idea of re-birth and another life is ever present in a corner of his sub-conscious. For the common man, the phantom of the next life and fear of reaping the consequences of wrong acts keep haunting him and stirring his conscience. This acts as a self-regulatory mechanism to keep him off the wrong track.

The over all Hindu view of religion has been well described by J. Krishna Murthy. He says that religion is a pathless land in which each individual has to find his own path. That is, every one has to work out his own salvation in a manner he deems fit. No individual or religious organization can claim copy right to the words of God. This widest possible view of religion implicit in Hinduism sets it quite apart from other organized religions of the world. It also makes it the only religious system in the world which sets its follower completely free to live his religious and worldly life in his own best way.

Viewed in historical perspective, freedom of the individual in religious and temporal matters is of revolutionary significance. For, the history of civilization is essentially the history of freedom of the individual from the clutches of the group - be it the village community, tribe or religious establishment. Ever since man started living in society, he had been a slave to either of these groups or collectivities. As the famous French revolutionary thinker, Rousseau observed, "Man is born free but is every where in chains". While village community lost its hold on the individual at the end of the feudal era and tribes have become insignificant except in some backward regions, religion still has a strong grip over individuals in large parts of the world. In fact, there is an upsurge of religious revivalism in the Islamic world (Al Quida, Taliban and 'clash of civilizations'). It represents a lapse into the medieval syndrome of strong grip of religion on the individual. In such a back-drop of regression into medievalism in the Muslim world, Hinduism's 'mantra' of individual freedom brings about a whiff of modernism on the troubled world.

In that sense, Hinduism stands out as the most modern religious system in the world. This has not only assured its survival in the modern age but also made some of its key spiritual concepts and practices acceptable across the board in the modern world. The Bhakti movement of Krishna consciousness has many takers in the Western world whose number is growing. Another more notable gift of Hinduism to the world is the technique of 'Yoga' as a means of betterment of human life. Originally conceived as a means of achieving salvation through spiritual discipline and dedication, 'yoga' has assumed a worldlier dimension in modern times as a mode of physical and mental well-being of man.

Originating in the 'Yoga Sutra' of the celebrated grammarian Patanjali, yoga involves various stages of mental and physical posturing culminating in 'Samadhi', that is, deep meditation. These include sitting in a certain posture, the most famous being 'Padmasana' or lotus posture, control of breath known as 'Pranayama', steadying the mind by concentrating on a single object or a sacred symbol, and deep meditation when the whole personality is dissolved merging into the object of concentration. The physical and mental experiences of 'yoga' have been widely accepted the world over as being conducive to healthy living. The 'yoga' exercises are being adopted into practice by more and more people regardless for their formal religious identity.

At the same time, the spiritual perception of 'yoga' as an integral part of Hindu theism remains intact. This has been eloquently described by a great apostle of modern Hinduism, Sri Aurobindo. He observes - "By 'Yoga' we can rise out of falsehood into truth, out of weakness into force, out of pain and grief into bliss, out of bondage into freedom, out of death into immortality, out of darkness into light........Out of Maya into God". ("The hour of God" by Sri Aurobindo, Sri Aurobindo Ashram, Pondicherry, second edition, 2006). Sri Aurobindo, it may be noted, perfected the practice of yoga as a spiritual endeavour to connect with God in his own life time and attracted disciples from all over the World. An idyllic habitat named "Auroville" after him, located in a thinly forested area a few miles away from Pondicherry, has come to be a hub of his devout followers mostly from western countries, besides Indians. And the centre of attraction in the habitat is a fully modern meditation hall known as 'Matri Sadan' after the holy Mother, a French national originally who was a yogi herself and remained as Sri Aurobindo's shadow during his life as a yogi.

As an offshoot of yoga, Transcendental Meditation, a method of detaching oneself from problems, anxiety, etc. by silent meditation, is a specific gift of Hinduism to modern society. In late 1960's, the 'Beatles' who revolted against the crass materialism of the western world, took to Transcendental Meditation in a big way to be at peace with themselves and their flawed world. It is sought after today by people from different parts of the world for relief and solace from the fast pace and vagaries of modern life. Like yoga in general, transcendental meditation is being acknowledged as a unique contribution to human happiness in modern world.

In this post-modern age when religion itself is under clouds, some receding into fundamentalism and obscurantism while others being assailed by all manners of rationalists, Hinduism is holding on to its own by virtue of its singular contributions to the well-being of humanity. In this way, the oldest living religion in the world has also come to be the most modern one. That is the wonder that is Hinduism.

Bibliography

The list includes many books studied earlier from which copious notes had been taken in normal course. These books provided a suitable background for my further studies undertaken for writing of this book. And the notes taken from them proved to be very useful in course of my writing.

- *A Study of History,* Arnold J. Toynbee, (Abridgement of Volumes I to IV by D.C. Somervell.)
- *Hellenism: The History of a Civilisation,* Arnold J. Toynbee.
- *Roman Britain,* R.G. Collingwood and J.N.L. Myres.
- *The Hellenistic World,* F.W. Walbank.
- *Glimpses of World History,* Jawaharlal Nehru.
- *The Oxford History of India,* Vincent A. Smith,

  Edited by Percival Spear, 1958.
- *A History of Political Thought,* Plato to Burke, S.P. Singh,1967.
- *Modern Indian Political Thought,* V.P. Verma, 1978.
- *History of Medieval India,* V.D. Mahajan, 10th Edition, 2005.
- *A Short History of the Muslim Rule in India,* Ishwari Prasad, 1982.
- *History of India - 1000 - 1707,* A.L. Srivastava, 1984.
- *Early Medieval India,* A.B. Pandey, 1977.
- *A History of India,* Romila Thapar.

- *A History of South India,* Nilkanta Sastri, 1966.
- *The Wonder that was India,* A.L. Basham.
- *The Continent of Circe,* Nirad C. Chowdhuri, 1965.
- *Hinduism: A Religion to live By,* Nirad C. Chowdhuri,1979.
- *A Short History of Hinduism,* Klaus K. Klostermaier, 2006.
- *History of Dharamasastra,* P.V. Kane, 1953.
- *Conversation with Nehru,* Tibor Mande, 1958.
- *Twelfth Book of 'Mahabharata'* entitled 'Shanti Parva'.
- *The Gita,* with Hindi translation Published by the Gita Press, Gorakhpur.
- *Karma Yoga* (of Gita), Swami Vivekananda, 1984.
- *Anasakti Yoga* (Interpretation of Gita), Mahatma Gandhi.
- *Samanvaya Yoga* (Interpretation of Gita in Hindi), Dr. Ram Chandra Pradhan, 1993.
- *Bhagvad Gita* : A Primer, Dr. Ram Chandra Pradhan, 1995.
- *Ramayan,* Published by Gita Press, Gorakhpur.
- *Rig Veda* (in Hindi), Radha Krishna Srimali.
- *Kena Upanishad,* with the commentary of Shankaracharya, Translated by Swami Gambhirananda, 1981.
- *Isopanishad, with Introduction and translation* by Swami Prabhupada, Founder of ISCON,1997.
- *The Condensed Gospel of Sri Rama Krishna,* published by Ram Krishna Math, Madras (now Chennai), 1978.
- *The Mind of Adi Shankarcharya,* Y. Keshava Menon, 2005.
- *The life of Vivekananda and Universal Gospel,* Romain Rolland, Fourth Impression, 1953.
- *Vivekananda:* A Biography, Swami Nikhilananda, 1964.
- *In Defence of Hinduism,* Swami Vivekananda, Twelfth Impression, 1999.
- *The Life of Sri Aurobindo,* A.B. Purani, Fourth edition, 1978.
- *Twelve Years with Sri Aurobindo,* Nirodbaran, Third edition, 1988.

- *The Hour of God,* Sri Aurobindo, Nirodbaran, Third edition, 1988.
- *The Riddle of this World,* 6th edition, 1973.
- *The Philosophy of the Upanishads,* Sri Aurobindo, 2nd edition, 2003.
- *Gita Darshan* - 12 (in Hindi), Swami Niranjanand Saraswati, 2nd edition 1997.
- *Bharat Ki Sant Parampara,* Dr. Krishna Gopal, 2004.
- *Worship Yourself: Life and Message of Aghoreshwar* Bhagwan Ram, S. Sahay, 1996.
- *Amar Vani* (Hindi), B.K. Tripurari Verma.
- *Vedanta Kusum,* Swami Abhayananda Saraswati, 2005.
- *A Short Life of Sri Rama Krishna,* Sami Tejasananda, 20th Impression, 2003.
- *Gurvayupura Purana,* a part of Nardiya Purana, one of the Maha Purana of Vaishnava tradition.
- *The Concept of Hindu Nation,* Abhas Chatterjee, 1995.
- *The Argumentative Indian:* Writings on Indian History, Culture and Identity, Amartya Sen, 2005.
- *The Dawning of the Theosophical Movement,* Michael Gomes, 1987.
- *New Catholic Edition of the Holy Bible,* Catholic Book Publishing Company, New York.
- *The Book* (An exhaustive translation of the Bible in present day idioms), Tyndale House Publishers, Wheaton, U.S.A.
- *Jesus lived in India: His unknown Life before and after crucifixion,* Holger Kresten, 2001.
- *The Life of Rama Krishna,* Romain Rolland.
- *The Story of My Experiment with Truth,* Mahatma Gandhi, 1929.
- *Collected works of Mahatma Gandhi* (Selected Parts).
- *The Clash of Civilisations and the Remaking of world order,* Samuel P. Huntington, 1996.
- *A History of India,* Percival Spear, 1968.

- *India's Struggle for Independence,* Bipan Chandra and others.
- *Freedom at Midnight,* Larry Collins and Dominique Lappierre, 1976.
- *India from Curzon to Nehru and after,* Durga Das, 1971.
- *Bunch of Thoughts,* M.S. Golwalkar, Sahitya Singhu Prakashan, Bangalore, 2000.
- *Shri Sain Amritputra* (Hindi), Sain Publications, Nagpur.
- *Sat Ki Vani Sat Ki Jabani* (Hindi), Sain Publications, Nagpur.
- *Devi Bhagwata Purana* (English Translation).
- *Annie Besant, The Theosophic Life* (Theosophical Publishing House, Chennai), 1984.
- Embree, Ainslie T., ed. *Sources of Indian Tradition.* Vol. 1: *From the Beginning to 1800.* 2nd ed. New York: Columbia University Press, 1988.
- Herman, A. L., A BriefIntroduction to Hinduism: Religion, Philosophy, and Ways of Liberation. Boulder, Colo.: Westview, 1991.
- Hopkins, Thomas J. *The Hindu Religious Tradition.* Encino, Calif.: Dickenson, 1971.
- Kinsley, David R. *Hinduism: A Cultural Perspective.* 2nd ed. Englewood Cliffs, N.J.: Prentice Hall, 1993.
- Klostermaier, Klaus K. *A Survey of Hinduism.* Albany: State University of New York Press, 1989.
- *The Laws of Manu.* Translated by Wendy Doniger, with Brian K. Smith. London, New York: Penguin Books, 1991.
- Bromley, David and Larry Shinn. *Krishna Consciousness in the West.* Lewisburg: Bucknell University Press, 1989.
- Burke, Mary Louise. *Swami Vivekananda in America: New Discoveries.* Calcutta: Advaita Ashrama, 1966.
- Eck, Diana L. *Darsan: Seeing the Divine Image in India.* New York: Columbia University Press, 1995.
- Eck, Diana L. "New Age Hinduism in America," in Nathan and Sulochana Glazer, eds. *Conflicting Images: India and the United States.* Glenndale, Maryland: Riverdale, 1990.

- Hay, Stephen N. "Rabindranath Tagore in America," *American Quarterly*. 14 (Fall 1962), 439-63.
- Jackson, Carl T. *The Oriental Religions and American Thought: Nineteenth-Century Explorations*. Westport, Conn.: Greenwood Press, 1981.
- Jensen, Joan M. *Passage from India: Asian Indians in North America*. New Haven: Yale University Press.
- Ramaswamy, Sunita and Sundar. *Vedic Heritage Teaching Program* (3 Vols.) Saylorsburg, PA: Arsha Vidya Gurukulam.
- Tejomayananda, Swami. *Hindu Culture: An Introduction*. Piercy, CA: Chinmaya Publications, 1993.
- Unverzagt, Eric. "Paramahansa Yogananda and Self-Realization Fellowship 1920-1994: A History and Reflection on Non-Western Teachings." Harvard Divinity School Paper, 1993.
- Viswanathan, Ed. *Am I a Hindu? The Hinduism Primer*. San Francisco: Halo Books, 1992.
- Vivekananda, Swami. *Raja Yoga*. New York: Ramakrishna - Vivekananda Center, 1973.
- Vivekananda Vedanta Society, *Vedanta in Chicago: Golden Jubilee Souvenir*. Chicago: Vivekananda Vedanta Society, 1981.
- Walters, Donald. *The Path: Autobiography of a Western Yogi (Swami Kriyananda)*. Nevada City: Ananda Publications, 1977.
- C. N. E. Eliot, *Hinduism and Buddhism* (3 Vol., 1921; repr. 1968).
- A. B. Keith, The Religion and Philosophy of the Veda and Upanishads (1925, repr. 1971).
- S. Radhakrishnan, The Hindu View of Life (1927, repr. 1962).
- L. Renou, *Religions of Ancient India* (1953, repr. 1968) and *Hinduism* (1961).
- R. G. Zaehner, *Hinduism* (1962).

- A. T. Embree, ed., *The Hindu Tradition* (1966, repr. 1972).
- T. J. Hopkins, The Hindu Religious Tradition (1971).
- P. H. Ashby, Modern Trends in Hinduism (1974).
- A. L. Basham, The Origins and Development of Classical Hinduism (1989).
- Vasudha Dalmia and Heinrich Von Stietencron (edited).Representing Hinduism: The Construction of Religious and National Identity. New Delhi: Sage Publications, 1995.
- *Hinduism and Modernity.* David Smith. Oxford: Blackwell, 2003.
- *Hinduism: Past and Present,* Axel Michaels. Translated by Barbara Harshaw. Princeton University Press.
- *Awaken Bharata: A Call For India's Rebirth.* David Frawley, American Institute of Vedic Studies, New Mexico.
- Bruce M. Sullivan, *A to Z of Hinduism,* Vision Books.
- R V Bhasin, *Essence of Hinduism,* Jaico.
- Steven J. Rosen, *Essential Hinduism,* Pentagon Press, 2008.
- Sen, K.M., *Hinduism,* Penguin.
- K. Satchidananda Murthy, *Hinduism and its Development,* D K Printworld Pvt. Ltd., 2007.
- Krishan Saigal, *God and Goddesses in Hinduism,* Kalpaz Publications, 2007.
- Gunther-Dietz Sontheimer & Hermann Kulke (ed.), *Hinduism Reconsidered,* Manohar, 2001.
- Prem P. Bhalla, *Hindu Gods & Goddesses,* Pustak Mahal, 2007.
- Satguru Sivaya Subramuniyaswami, *How to Become a Hindu: A Guide for Seekers and Born Hindus,* Motilal Banarsidass.
- Swami Ramashankar Das, *Encyclopaedia of Indian Mythology,* Anmol Publications Pvt. Ltd., 2007.
- Vasudha Dalmia & Heinrich von Stietencron (ed.), *The Oxford India Hinduism Reader,* Oxford University Press, 2007.

- Akshoy K. Majumdar, *The Hindu History,* Rupa & Co., 2008.
- Renou, Louis (editor), *Hinduism,* George Braziller, New York, 1962,
- Zaehner, R. C.; *Hinduism,* Oxford University Press, 1985.
- Adeep Sen, Encyclopaedia of Religion, Anmol Publications, 2006.
- E.T. Sankaran Kutty, *A Glimpse on Vedic Concepts,* Bharatiya Vidya Bhavan, 2006.
- Harold Coward, Sin and Salvation in the World Religions, Viva Books, 2007.
- Swami Harshananda, The Ten Cardinal Upanisads: A Brief Study, Ramakrishna Math, 1998.
- Madhusudan Pati, *Bhagavad Gita: A Literary Elucidation,* Popular Prakashan, 1997.
- Capra, Fritjof, The Tao of Physics, Flamingo/Fontana, 1988.
- John Dowson, A Classical Dictionary of Hindu Mythology and Religion: Geography, History and Literature, Pilgrims Book House, 2006.
- Christopher Key Chapple, *Hinduism and Ecology: The Intersection of Earth, Sky and Water,* Oxford University Press.
- Dubois J. A. Abbe, *Hindu manners, customs and ceremonies,* The Clarendon Press, Great Britain 1959.
- Radhakrishnan, *The Hindu View of Life. The Upton lectures of 1926*, George Allan and Unwin Ltd, Great Britain 1957.
- Anil Kumar Dwivedi, *Encyclopaedia of Indian Customs & Rituals,* Anmol Publications Pvt. Ltd., 2007.
- R. Kumar & S. Ram, *Encyclopaedia of Hinduism,* Crescent Publishing Corporation, 2007.
- Margaret Stutley, *Hindu Deities: A Mythological Dictionary with Illustrations,* Munshiram Manoharlal Publishers, 2006.

Index

B

I

J

K

N

O

P